THE FICTION OF
BHABANI BHATTACHARYA

THE FICTION OF
BHABANI BHATTACHARYA

KH. KUNJO SINGH

ATLANTIC
PUBLISHERS & DISTRIBUTORS

Published by
ATLANTIC PUBLISHERS AND DISTRIBUTORS
B-2, Vishal Enclave, Opp. Rajouri Garden, New Delhi-27
Phones : 5413460, 5429987, 5466842

Sales Office
4215/1, Ansari Road, Darya Ganj, New Delhi-02
Phones : 3273880, 3285873, 3280451
Fax : 91-11-3285873
web : www.atlanticbooks.com
e-mail : info@atlanticbooks.com

ISBN 81-269-0183-7

Typeset at
APD Computer Graphics, Delhi
Printed in India at
Nice Printing Press, Delhi

Dedicated to

My revered grandmother
Late Smt. Kh. Tomcha Devi
Under whose careful protection
I enjoyed my pupilhood

PREFACE

Indo-Anglian Literature has become popular by forming an integral part of English literature and by reflecting and echoing events of great importance and significance in the history of India. The attainment of Independence is the greatest event in modern Indian history. The period preceding this event was packed with political struggle, suffering and hope, but the period following it was full of unexpected trials and turmoils. In the midst of these stresses and strains many valiant efforts have been made to create a new order.

The book entitled *The Fiction of Bhabani Bhattacharya* studies the more remarkable political novels of eminent Indian novelists. It makes a thorough and objective study of the celebrated novelist Bhabani Bhattacharya's novels, constituting a social document of post-Independence India.

The book has been prepared under the able and loving supervision of Dr. K.K. Chatterjee, Professor of English, Manipur University, Canchipur. So, I am deeply beholden to the esteemed supervisor of mine for his constant encouragement and perennial source of suggestions which made the completion of my book possible within three years.

I am indebted to the authorities of the following libraries for their generous and prompt services: the Manipur University Library, Canchipur; the C.I.E. & F.L., Regional Centre Library, Shillong; the Gauhati University Library, Guwahati; the National Library, Kolkata and the N.L.S. College Library, Nambol.

I am grateful to Dr. N. Khagendra Singh, Dean, School of Humanities, Manipur University for his kind suggestions towards the undertaking and completion of the book in time.

I acknowledge my indebtedness to my Senior Colleague, Shri Ch. Iboton Singh, Head of Department of English, N.L.S. College, Nambol, for providing an invaluable stimulation and generous help through several personal discussions and conversations.

I am also grateful to Dr. G.S. Balarama Gupta, Editor, *The Journal of Indian Writing in English*, Gulbarga, for sending to me all the back numbers of the JIWE publications when they were very much needed and for his kind suggestions and encouragement in my endeavour to prepare this work.

I express my gratitude to M/s Writers Workshop, Calcutta for providing me with all the books I needed out of their publications.

I also do not forget to thank Dr. S.C. Saha, Vice-Chancellor, Assam University, Silchar and formerly Associate Professor of English, Manipur University for his constant encouragement and useful suggestions towards the completion of my work.

I am particularly thankful to Mr. A. Deben Singh, Steno-typist, Department of English, Manipur University for his kind and invaluable help in typing this work within a short time.

I express my gratitude and thanks to my loving wife Mrs. Memcha Devi for her great and unforgettable help in various ways in the completion this study.

Last but not the least, my thanks are also due to M/s Atlantic Publishers and Distributors, B-2, Vishal Enclave, opposite Rajouri Garden, New Delhi, India for undertaking the publication of this book successfully within a short time.

KH. KUNJO SINGH

Contents

Introduction

Bhabani Bhattacharya, the earliest of the social realists of post-Independence Indian English fiction, is a well-known Indo-Anglian novelist. His books have been translated in more than two dozen foreign languages, sixteen of which are European and he has attained a world-wide renown. The coveted Sahitya Akademi award to him in 1967 for his fifth novel, *Shadow from Ladakh,* is a fitting recognition of his standing and achievement in Indian English fiction.

Under the strange coincidences of being a Bengali, born in 1906 in Bhagalpur town in Bihar, writing in an alien language and living in Nagpur in Maharashtra, he started his career as a freelance writer. With a doctorate degree from London University on historical research he worked for several years as press attache to the Indian Embassy in Washington. He travelled widely and was associated with a research centre at the University of Hawaii.

Bhattacharya is a novelist strongly influenced by the ideas of Tagore and Gandhi, while both his fictional theory and practice show his affinity with Mulk Raj Anand. He is a believer in the social character and significance of art and literature and believes that "Art must teach, but unobtrusively, by its vivid interpretation of life. Art must preach, but only by virtue of its being a vehicle of truth. If that is propaganda, there is no need to eschew the word."[1] Bhattacharya's view of art, however foreign to the aesthetically inclined writer in the West, is not at all uncharacteristic in modern Indian literature with its intense socio-political consciousness. He is a novelist of ideas, not of art. He writes for instruction, not for entertainment. Aesthetically,

Bhattacharya was insensitive and he rarely wrote in an idiomatic English, a language made great by literary masters.

Bhattacharya once remarked that "a novel must have a social purpose. It must place before the reader something from the society's point of view. Art is not necessarily for art's sake. Purposeless art and literature which is much in vogue does not appear to me to be a sound judgement."[2] All his novels present a true picture of India and its teeming millions. His outlook is highly constructive and purposeful.

Smt. Lila Ray writes: "As we read his writing, we hear the dialogue between man and his situation, between man and man and between man and the ideas he lives by."[3] High idealism permeates his works and they record the hopes and aspirations of people heroically involved in the struggle between the old and the new and inspired by the vision of a just social order. He portrays full-blooded men and women, creatures of their society, victims of its unjust persecutions and yet possessing inevitable strength to carry the banner of the ideals of a new India. He faithfully and soberly depicts the horrors characteristic of alien rule and the old mode of life; he portrays the grandeur of the peasant and the downtrodden and their role in remaking the motherland, the dream of the Indian nationalist.

Bhattacharya's works consist of translations from Tagore, entitled *The Golden Boat, Indian Cavalcade,* a collection of historical sketches; *Towards Universal Man,* a commemoration volume published on the eve of the birth centenary of Tagore; *Steel Hawk,* a collection of fifteen short stories; *Gandhi, the Writer: The Image as It Grew,* a highly stimulating and provocative study released on the occasion of the birth centenary of Mahatma Gandhi and, what is more important, six novels—*So Many Hungers*! (1947); *Music for Mohini* (1952); *He Who Rides a Tiger* (1954); *A Goddess Named Gold* (1960); *Shadow from Ladakh* (1966) and *A Dream in Hawaii* (1978). These six novels may be grouped into the following three categories (according to their thematic structure but not according to their year of writing or publication):

1. Rural Novels

The first novel *So Many Hungers*! was set against the background of the Quit India Movement and the Bengal Famine of 1943. It deals with the theme of exploitation—political, economic and social. The "so many hungers" of the title hints at different kinds of hungers— (i) for political freedom (in the case of India); (ii) for imperial expansion (in the case of the axis powers); (iii) for money (in the case of the capitalists who create artificial famine by hoarding rice); (iv) for food (in the case of the starved Bengali poor); (v) for sex (in the case of the sex-starved soldiers one of whom rapes the destitute rustic girl Kajoli); (vi) for human dignity and self-respect (in the case of Kajoli who rejects prostitution even though she is starving) and (vii) the hunger as a spiritual weapon employed by the freedom fighters (in the case of Devata's fast unto death in jail). Its main theme is hunger for food and the novelist gives a detailed, graphic and moving picture of the hunger and heavy loss of human lives resulting from it.

He Who Rides a Tiger, the third novel in the chronology of publication deals with an attack on both those who profited by people's misery during the famine and those who exploited them as caste tyrants. The novel discusses a variation on the theme of hunger. With a fascinating beginning, the story runs rapidly surging with emotion and agitation. It is a grim satire on Hindu orthodoxy telling the story of Kalo, a poor blacksmith, who, jailed for stealing a bunch of bananas, vows revenge on society. He makes a living for himself and his daughter by faking a miracle—a miracle that begins as a fraud and ends as a legend—and passing himself off as a Brahmin Priest. The story ends with a note of triumph for the soul over the flesh. There is an intricate criss-cross of themes here such as the conflict between appearance and reality, the haves and the have-nots, and religious hypocrisy. The novel is based on the ancient saying— "He who rides a tiger" cannot dismount.

2. Social Novels

Music for Mohini, the second of his novels, moves on two levels—on the personal level, the city-bred, village-wed girl Mohini's adjustment to her new life style and on the social level, the story of the old Eastern view of life connecting with the new semi-Western outlook, an attempt to wed the 'horoscope' with the 'microscope.' The representative of the old Eastern view of life is Jayadev, a quiet scholar and villager, while the new semi-Western outlook is represented by his wife Mohini. The psychological interest of the novel lies in the opposition between Jayadev and his excessively conservative mother. She is impressed, at last, by the works of her son and daughter-in-law and the value of changes they bring to the village and so she is prepared to give up her resistance to all their modernising works.

The fourth novel *A Goddess Named Gold* is beautiful a novel on Indian social life and a masterly satire on those who live by the lure of gold. Meera's grandfather, a wandering minstrel, gives her an amulet (*taveez*) telling that it will turn the base metals into gold if she does an act of real kindness. She rescues a child. Seth Samsunderji seeks to profit out of India's new found freedom and enters into a business deal with Meera on a fifty-fifty basis. Disgusted with the amulet as it does not work properly, Meera throws it into the river. Luckily the minstrel comes back and tells the people that "freedom," not the *taveez*, is the real touchstone.

The fifth novel *Shadow from Ladakh* contrasts the Gandhism of Satyajit Sen of Gandhigram with the Scientism of Bhaskar, Chief Engineer of Steeltown. The novel provides an insight into the contrasting contemporary life of India symbolised by Satyajit who regards Indian village life as the ideal life and by the Westernised American trained Bhaskar, the forward-looking Chief Engineer in a steel plant, who feels India's future lies in industrialisation. It ends on a weak note of coexistence of these two ideologies. Bhaskar wants to dispossess Gandhigram, because it is a hindrance to India's industrialisation. The novel is characteristic of Bhattacharya's thematic writing and works out a preconceived idea but in an artistic manner.

3. Novel of the Philosophico-cultural Duality of East and West

The latest novel *A Dream in Hawaii* deals with the theme of East-West encounter. This time, the scene is laid in Hawaii, no better meeting ground of East and West. While the East with all its spirituality has not yet completely mastered the flesh, the West continues to remain commercialised and confused. The East is represented by Swami Yogananda who is not above his love for Debjani and the two facets of American culture are represented by the two Americans—Dr. Swift, the organisational man, who wants to use Yogananda as a tool in founding a flourishing spiritual centre, and Dr. Gregson, the champion of the permissive society. Bhattacharya is found to resist the temptation to accept a ready-made solution at the end, though the Americans seem to be uniformly "flat" characters.

Bhattacharya's sense of situation and mastery of the narrative mode, the realism of his locale, his judicious use of Indianisms and his easily identifiable character types have perhaps created a picture of India which fits in admirably with pre-conceived foreign notions about this country. He has the vision of a Welfare Society at heart. His concerns are political, economic and social. He follows the tradition of European social realism. But one notable weakness in his art is the lack of depth in his treatment of problems in human relations and his distinctive quality lies also there: his aim is to create the novel of ideas in the Indian setting and make some meaning out of the experience of colonialism. The significance of his novel does not lie in its story or plot, but in its being a vehicle of the political philosophy of Indian nationalism, especially of that phase associated with the idealists, Vivekananda, Tagore and Mahatama Gandhi, so much so that his novels often read like essays. His novels are often obtrusively pre-occupied with the propagation of some sentimental notion or political idea. But we have to view this drawback in the context of the Indo-Anglian fiction in general.

REFERENCES

1. "Literature and Social Reality," *The Aryan Path*, XXVI, No. 9, Sept. 1955.
2. Sudhakar Joshi, "An Evening with Bhabani," *The Sunday Standard*, 27 April, 1969, Vol. 1.
3. Lila Ray, "Bhabani Bhattacharya: A Profile" *Indian Literature*, Vol. XI, No. 2, April-July 1968, 73-76.

1

Indo-Anglian Ficiton: A Brief Survey

Significance of the Term "Indo-Anqlian Literature"

The bulk of writing in English that came out as the by-product of an eventful encounter between Britain, vigorous and enterprising, and India, stagnant and chaotic, in the late eighteenth century and early part of the nineteenth century has been designated variously, from time to time as "Indo-Anglian Literature," "Indian Writing in English" and "Indo-English Literature." This variation in the nomenclature led to the confusion of interpretation between categories of writing such as "Anglo-Indian Literature," "Literature in the Indian Language translated into English" and "Original Composition in English by Indians." So E.F. Oaten includes and interprets Henry Derozio's poetry and the poetry of Toru Dutt, Sarojini Naidu, R. Tagore and Aravindo Ghose in the same category of Anglo-Indian Literature.

The same is the case with Bhupal Singh's interpretation in his *Survey of Anglo-Indian Fiction* (1934). Again, V.K. Gokak, in his book *English in India: Its Present and Future* (1964) interprets the term "Indo-Anglian Literature" as comprising the work of Indian writers in English and "Indo-English Literature" as consisting of translations by Indians from Indian literature into English."[1] K.R. Srinivasa Iyengar, in his book *Indian Writing in English* (1962) includes English translations of Tagore's novels and plays done by others in the category of Indian creative writing in English, while the same is excluded by H.M. Williams from his *Indo-Anglian Literature 1800-1970: A Survey* (1976).

Besides, the term "Indo-English Literature" is used to mean literature produced by Indians in English in John B. Alphonso Karkala's—*Indo-English Literature in the Nineteenth Century* (1970).

But the term "Indo-Anglian Literature" was coined by J.H. Cousins in connection with the *Specimen Compositions from Native Students,* published in Calcutta in 1883. Again the term "Indo-Anglian" has not only become a considerably current term, but also has become a familiar and accepted term to mean Indian contribution to literature in English after the publication of Dr. K.R. Srinivasa Iyengar's two admirable books—*Indo-Anglian Literature* (1943) and *Indian Writing in English* (1962). In this regard Mulk Raj Anand also remarks: "This has come to be known as Indo-Anglian writing and has been quite an active school of didactic and creative art for at least a century."[2] Thus, the story of Indo-Anglian Literature and consequently that of Indo-Anglian Fiction is the story of only about one and a half century from today.

Growth of Indo-Anglian Fiction: A Panoramic Scene, upto 1920

Compared to poetry and drama prose fiction had a delayed start in the Indo-Anglian literature. The Earliest fictional works were tales rather than proper 'novels' and many were written at all for political theme such as Kylash Chunder Dutt's *A Journal of 48 hours of the year 1945* published in "The Calcutta Literary Gazette" on 6 June, 1835 dealing with an imaginary unsuccessful revolt against the British rule a hundred years later and Shoshee Chunder Dutt's *Republic of Orissa: Annals from the pages of the Twentieth Century* appeared in "Saturday Evening Hurkaru" on 25 May 1845 dealing with a fantastic British defeat and establishment of a democratic republic in Orissa. But the first Indian novel published in English was Bankim Chandra Chatterjee's (1834-94) *Rajmohan's Wife* serialised in the Calcutta Weekly, *The Indian Field* in 1864 (long before it appeared posthumously in proper book form in 1935). With a liberal use of Indian words and creating a local colour on a setting of an East Bengal village in the late 19th century, the novel narrates the story of a Hindu wife, Matangini and her long suffering in the hands of her husband Rajmohan.

But before the turn of the 19th century surprisingly novels by four women novelists appeared in the scene of the Indo-Anglian fiction. They are: Raj Lakshmi Debi's *The Hindoo Wife* or *The Enchanted Fruit* (Calcutta, 1876); Toru Dutt's unfinished novel, *Bianca or The Young Spanish Maiden* (Calcutta, 1878); Krupabai Satthianadhan's *Kamala: A Story of Hindu Life* (Madras & Bombay, 1895) and *Saguna: A Story of Native Christian Life* (Madras & Bombay, 1895) and Shevantibai M. Nikambe's *Ratanbai: A Sketch of a Bombay High Caste Hindu Young Wife* (London, 1895).

Then appeared Ramkrishna Punt's *The Boy of Bengal* (Philadelphia, 1866); Tarachand *Mukerjea's The Scorpions or the Eastern Thoughts* (Allahabad, 1868), Lal Behari Day's *Govinda Samanta* or *The History of a Bengal Raiyat* (London, 1874); *Gowry, An Indian Village Girl* by an anonymous author (Madras, 1876), Anand Prasad Dutt's *The Indolence* (Calcutta, 1878); Shoshee Chunder Dutt's *The Young Zamindar* (London, 1883); Trailokya Nath Das's *Hirimba's Wedding* (Midnapore, 1884); Mirza Moorad Alee Beg's *Lalun, the Beragun*, or *The Battle of Panipat* (Bombay, 1864); Sanjihi Mull's *The Interesting Story of Prince Poorun* (Delhi, 1886); M. Dutt's *Bijoy Chand: An Indian Tale* (Calcutta, 1900); *Kamarupa and Kamalatha* (Calcutta, 1889) by an anonymous author; Jogendranath Chattopadhyaya's *The Girl and Her Tutor* (Bhagalpur, 1891); and B. Rajam Iyer's *True Greatness of Vasudeva Sastri* published in book form in 1925 at London.

Then there came the period of Romesh Chunder Dutt's translated novels *The Lake of Palms: A Story of Indian Domestic Life* (London, 1902); *The Slave Girl of Agra, An Indian Historical Romance* (London, 1909); and Sarath Kumar Ghosh's *Verdict of the Gods* (New York,1905); later published under the title,

1001 Indian Nights: The Trials of Narayan Lal (London, 1906); *The Prince of Destiny: The New Krishna* (London, 1909). Then appeared novels of Madras novelists Madhviah's *Thillai Gorvindan* (London, 1916) showing a beautiful account of the mental development of a contemporary South Indian Brahmin youth; *Clarinda* (Madras, 1915); *Nanda, the Pariah Who Overcame Caste* (Madras, 1923) and Lt. Panju's—*A Modern Indian* (Madras, 1924). Next T. Ramakrishna Pillai wrote *Padmini* (London, 1903) dealing with the story of a village maiden's preference of a high-souled lover to an aristocratic usurper and *A Dive for Death* (London, 1911) dealing with the story of the discovery of an obscure youth loved by a princess to be a long-lost prince. Next came out Punjabi Sirdar Jogendra Singh's realistic social fictions: *Nur Jahan, The Romance of an Indian Queen* (1909); *Nasrin, An Indian Medley* (1911); *Kamala* (1925) and *Kamini* [sic] (1931).

Mention may be made of the coming out of S.T. Ram's *Cosmopolitan Hinduani* (Lahore, 1902); M. Venkatesiya Naidu's *The Princess Kamala* or *The Model Wife* (Madras, 1904); S.M. Mitra's *Hindupore: A Peep Behind the Indian Unrest: An Anglo-Indian Romance* (London, 1909); Balkrishna's *Man of Letters* (Calcutta, 1911); M.M. Munshi's *Beauty and Joy* (Surat, 1914); Svarna Kumari Ghosal's *The Fatal Garland* (N.Y., 1915); T.R. Krishnaswami's *Selma: A Tale of the Times of Old* (Madras, 1916); T.K. Gopal Panikkar's *Storm and Sunshine* (Calicut, 1916); Srinivasa Rau's *Varanasi: The Portuguese Ambassador* (Bezwada, 1917); C. Parthasarathy's *Sangili Karuppan* or *The Wheel of Destiny* (Vellore, 1920).

Indo-Anglian Novels (1920-1947)

The period of 1920-1947 which is really the period of Gandhian movement, made a definite impact on the novelists and influenced their outlook on theme and characterisation. The earliest novel written under the influence of Gandhian philosophy was K.S. Venkataramani's *Murugan, The Tiller* (1927) contrasting the careers of two young South Indian friends Kedari, a materialist ruined by his own chicanery, and Ramu, an introvert, who founded an ideal rural colony on Gandhian principles at the end of the novel. His second novel *Kandan, the Patriot: A Novel of New India in the Making* (1932)deals with the story of Kandan's resignation from the Indian Civil Service to plunge into the freedom struggle, finally succumbing to a police bullet. Then came out *Baladitya* (1930) by A.S.P. Ayyar telling the story of Baladitya, the king of Magadha and Yasodharman, the king of Mahakosala defeating the invading Huns. Ayyar's second novel *Three Men of Destiny* (1939) narrates the story of Alexander's invasion of India. The three men were—Alexander the great, Indian Emperor Chandragupta Maurya and his Brahmin Prime Minister Chanakya. Then there appeared Tamil novelist Krishnaswami Nagarjan's Galsworthian family chronicle *Athavar House* (1939) showing the complex family relationship and the clash between orthodoxy and modernism in one Brahmin Gopinath's family. It is discussed fully in Chapter 2 of this book where his later novel *Chronicles of Kedaram* (1961) is also discussed in detail.

The appearance of the major trio: Mulk Raj Anand, R.K. Narayan and Raja Rao with their first novels published in 1935, 1935 and 1938 respectively, on the scene of Indo-Anglian fiction is remarkable because each revealed in his own characteristic way, the various possibilities of Indo-Anglian fiction.

The eldest of the trio, Anand, was born in Peshawar in 1905, the son of a coppersmith turned soldier. He educated in the cantonment schools and the University of Punjab from where he graduated with an Honours degree and went to London for doing research in philosophy under Professor Dawes Hicks, the great Kantian scholar in 1924 and there he became interested in the study of Indian art. Participating in the Gandhian movement while at College, he suffered a brief imprisonment in London; he came in touch with the left wing politics and *avant garde* movements and joined the International Brigade during the Spanish Civil War. He returned home and became a leading cultural figure as the editor of the art magazine, *Marg* in Bombay.

Anand narrates the story of his upbringing in the autobiographical *Apology for Heroism* (1946). He gained his socialist faith from the European tradition and in most of his novels he deals with the persistent theme of humanism and humanitarian compassion for the social underdogs showing the picture of the urban proletariat, the low-castes and the peasantry.

Anand's first three novels *Untouchable* (1935), *Coolie* (1936) and *Two Leaves and a Bud* (1937) form a natural trio with one victim hero, in each of them, of the oppressed and doomed outcast-proletarian whose fate is symbolic of India under the Imperial Rule and of the workers exploited by Capitalism. *Untouchable* and *Coolie* are fully discussed in Chapter 2 of this book.

Two Leaves and a Bud (1937) is the story of a Punjabi peasant Gangu who, with his wife Sajani and his daughter Leila enlists himself as a labourer in the Assam tea plantations. There he is lured by fabulous promises and compelled to work in unhygienic conditions and near starvation. He is shot dead by a British Overseer, being caught trying to rape his daughter. In the trial that followed a white jury declared the Overseer not guilty. In this novel Anand rests his case against imperialism.

Then appeared Anand's ambitious trilogy—*The Village* (1939), *Across the Black Waters* (1941) and *The Sword and the Sickle* (1942) dealing with the life of a young Sikh peasant, Lal Singh. The first novel of the trio depicts life in a typical Punjabi village before the time of the World War-I, seen through the eyes of young Lal Singh who is both insider and outsider, as he finally turns a rebel against the village landlords and escapes to France. The second of the trilogy depicts Lal Singh's joining the army fighting in Flanders in World War-I and the last of the trilogy showing Lal Singh returning from a German prison, hobnobbing with Communists and ending up in prison again. These are discussed in full in Chapter 3 of this book.

Then appeared *The Big Heart* (1945)* dealing with the story of a young coppersmith Ananta, called "Big Heart" because of his generosity. He champions machines and modernity in a traditional society, a theme that would appear in Bhattacharya also, and finally pays the price with his life. The novel is the last of Anand's novels of social protest showing the catastrophic effect of capitalism on the Indian coppersmiths raising a luddite protest against the hated machines. The theme is ostensibly political.

Anand's *Seven Summers* (1951) narrating the story of his childhood, is the first volume of his proposed seven volume series of novels, *Seven Ages of Man,* a sort of semi-autobiographical series of novels dealing with the social, political and economic changes sweeping over India in the first quarter of this century with Krishan Chander as the protagonist. The next novel *Private Life of an Indian Prince* (1953), a political novel, is discussed in Chapter 2 of this book. *The Old Woman and the Cow* (1960) deals with the story of a cow-like submissive Gauri, a peasant girl driven out by her husband and sold to a rich merchant by her mother; her subsequent escape and her becoming self-reliant and final transformation into a veritable tigress. The novel is one more structural unit in the fabric of Anand's social vision.

The next novel of Anand, *The Road* (1961), is a short novel, reminding us of *Untouchable* and handling the same theme of untouchability some twenty-six years later. *The Death of a Hero* (1964) is also a short novel dealing with the story of Maqbool Sherwani crucified during the first invasion of Kashmir by Pakistani raiders in 1947. There appeared next another short novel, almost a long short story, *Lament On the Death of a Master of Arts* (1957) describing the last day of Nur, an unemployed M.A. suffering from consumption. But this novel exposes again

---

* The date of publication of *The Big Heart* is 1945 according to Dr. M.K. Naik whereas it is 1944 according to Prof. P.P. Mehta. But H.M. Williams records it to be 1948.

the weakness of Anand as a novelist. P.P. Mehta remarks: "This novelette suffers from a flimsy situation which is more pathetic than tragic in its unrestrained sentimentality and its loose plot."[3] The comment is just.

The second of the long series of autobiographical novels is *Morning Face* (1968), the first being *Seven Summers* in the projected series entitled *Seven Ages of Man*. The novel records the growth of the hero Krishan Chander from childhood through adolescence, his loves and hates, his tension and conflicts, his hopes and fears. It also shows the changes sweeping over the social life of the Punjab and the battling of social reforms, modernity and political consciousness with loyalty to the British Raj and orthodox conservatism. The next novel, *Confession of a Lover* (1976) is a sequel to his *Seven Summers* and *Morning Face*. The novel deals with Krishan Chander's going to college, his frustrated love-affair with a married Muslim girl, his plunging into the whirlpool of journalism and politics and his leaving for England at the end. The love story of Krishan and Yasmin, the bomb outrage and arrest of Krishan's first five years in U.K. will be the subject of *The Bubble,* the fourth novel in the ambitious *Seven Ages of Man*.

Anand also wrote short stories delineating the lives of the poorest of the poor, bottom dogs and "less miserables" of the Indian soil. These stories were collected in volumes like—*Barber's Trade Union and Other Stories* (1944); *The Tractor and the Corn Goddess* (1947); *Reflections on the Golden Bed and Other Stories* (1955); *Lajwanti,* etc. In all his novels and short stories Anand makes free use of Indian words and expletives to impart a realistic flavour to the speech of his characters. In spite of all possible limitations, Anand's fictional achievement is impossible with his wide range, living and realistic characters, and humanitarian compassion.

The second of the trio Rashipuram Krishnaswami Narayan, better known as R.K. Narayan, can be called the father of the regional novel in Indian Writing in English. He wrote no less than ten novels and hundred and fifty-one short stories about the imaginary town Malgudi and its surroundings. He was born in 1906 in Madras, the son of a school master, but he spent most of his life in Mysore city and came to novel writing from journalism. He wrote about middle class Indians engaged in a struggle to extricate themselves from the automatism of the past. His novels and short stories are full of sunshine and laughter, a happy, warm and compassionate humanity under whose shade eccentric individuals nurture their absurdities, a more imaginative world of fiction than Anand's.

R.K. Narayan's first novel *Swami and Friends* (1935) is a classical schoolboy story "of a child, written with complete objectivity with a humour strange to our fiction, closer to Chekhov than to any other English writer with the same underlying sense of beauty and sadness."[4] The novel deals with Swami, the hero and his friends Mani and Rajan. Swami is an average boy. The varied experiences of these three friends at Albert Mission School are described in a realistic vein. Narayan's mode of telling the story with a good understanding of a boy's mind makes the story interesting and lively against the background of Malgudi which is, for him, like Hardy's Wessex, a fictional universe.

Narayan's second novel *Bachelor of Arts* (1937) brought him considerable fame. It deals with the household of a South Indian Hindu family with Chandran, the son of Venkatachela Iyer, a retired District Judge of Malgudi, as the hero. The novel gives a true insight into a middle-class Hindu mind, manners and customs. Narayan's third novel, *The Dark Room* (1938) deals with the domestic disharmony in the family of Ramani, the father of Babu, Kamala and Sumati and the husband of Savitri. He is a branch manager of an Insurance Company who falls in love with Shanta Bai, a woman Insurance organiser. Savitri becomes miserable and from her attempt to commit suicide she is saved by a blacksmith. Returning home she resumes her normal duties as a housewife. The novel has a rather unconvincing end in the course of its movement from the normal to the abnormal and back to the normal again. None of the three characters Ramani, Savitri and Shanta Bai is significant and there is no emotional crisis in the novel except a weak storm in a little domestic tea-cup.

Narayan's next novel *The English Teacher* (1946) is the last novel before Independence. It deals with the life of Krishan, an English lecturer earning only a hundred rupees a month for his lecture to Indian students. He settles down with his wife Suseela and daughter Leela. His wife dies half-way through the book. In the second part of the book he establishes connection with the spirit of his dead wife and resolves to dedicate his remaining life to a children's school. It is a wonderfully painted miniature of India with vivid characters and landscapes. Suseela is depicted in the role of a devoted Hindu wife with steadfast attention to her domestic duties.

The next novel *Mr. Sampath* (1949) is a novel about a lovable rogue, Mr. Sampath, who is innocently crooked, cunningly foolish, unselfishly selfish and sadly cheerful. While shooting the climactic scene of a mythological film "Burning of Kama By Shiva's Third Eye," there are strange developments outside the official scenario, when Ravi, the young artist who has fallen in love with the actress Shanti, tries to carry her off. The action is crowded with eccentrics and the whole narrative is farcically coloured. It is an amusing novel with tragi-comic character, a good example of Narayan's novelistic preoccupation with the comic characteristics of life.

In his next novel *The Financial Expert* (1952) we are back to the town of Malgudi. The novel deals with the central character Margayya's dreams of wealth, his ambition to rise in social status, his innocent pride in his badly spoiled son and his inner confusion. He is cautious, shrewd, evasive, superstitious and self-confident. The novel is about the rise and fall of his fortune. He survives the fall and at the end is ready to start again under the banyan tree.

Narayan's next masterpiece *The Guide* (1958), winner of the Sahitya Akademi Award, 1960, is set against Malgudi surroundings. In it he achieves a *tour de force* in point of technique. The novel deals with the story of Raju, formerly a tourist guide who had been released from prison and has taken refuge in an old temple by the river. A peasant takes him for a priest and Raju helps the peasant to find a solution to his problems. This enables Raju to earn a reputation as a holy man. When a drought and a famine afflict the district, the people turn to him for help and he reluctantly accepts to propitiate the rain gods by fasting for fourteen days. It is at this point that he confesses to one of his followers that he is an imposter and gives a flash-back of his previous life, the tragi-comedy of his love for Rosie, the dancer, who was the wife of an unwordly scholar (for whose sake he had been jailed for a forgery in trying to prevent a possible reconciliation between her and her husband), and the rise and fall of his fortunes as a guide and a lover. After four days Raju dies in the true spirit of a saint.

The story of Raju falls into two parts, the past and the present. The past is told by Raju, the present, by the narrator (author). The past and the present are related by skilful plot construction. It is remarked thus :

> "The consistently braided time-scheme that is used in the novel contributes to a better and deeper understanding of the hero who is both a Swindler and a holyman. By alternating two time schemes at sharp intervals the author brings into focus those aspects of Raju's character which are essential for an understanding of his inner confusion."[5]

Another of Narayan's novels, *Waiting for the Mahatma* (1955), deals with the Gandhian freedom struggle, the Quit India Movement of 1942 and presents Mahatma Gandhi as a character while the Bharati-Sriram love story advances in the background. The novel closes with the close of Gandhi's life on January 30, 1948 and Chapter 2 of this book contains a clear discussion on the novel.

Narayan's *The Man-Eater of Malgudi* (1962) is a typical Malgudi novel dealing with how the happy days of Nataraj, a printer and of his friends are disturbed as Vasu, a taxidermist risen to ill-gotten affluence from humble beginnings, comes to be a lodger in his house. As Vasu has attempted to kill the temple elephant that Nataraj has befriended, to bag big game, tragi-comic complications arise. The elephant is saved where Vasu dies from his own demonically fierce fists in an attempt to kill a pair of mosquitoes settling on his forehead. Elements of suspense creep up into the story as the death is suspected to be a murder. But Vasu, to whom character is destiny, falls a victim to self-deception as Bhasmasura, the Rakshasa (demon) who, granted by Shiva the boon of reducing to ashes anyone he touched on the head, was finally tricked by Vishnu (disguised as a beautiful damsel-Mohini) into touching himself to death. Thus the novel parodies the self-immolation of the legendary monster, Bhasmasura. H.M. Williams remarks that "the whole book is a comic allegory of India with its conflicting traditions of epic violence accompanied by endless speechifying and dreaming."[6]

The Vendor of Sweets (1967) is a political novel with its humorous overtones. There is a continuation of Gandhian motif in it. The Gandhian sweet vendor Jagan's son Mali who is lured away by the West, returns from the U.S.A. with a half-American and half-Korean girl and plans for marketing a novel writing machine. This makes his father Jagan frustrated and renounce the world. In this novel Jagan is presented as a true disciple of Mahatma Gandhi. The action of the novel raises the questions of the clash of generations, of East-West confrontation and of the efficacy of Gandhism in the modern world.

The Painter of Signs (1976) serialised in the July- September issues of "The Illustrated Weekly of India" deals with the relation of Raman, a young sign painter and Daisy of the Family Planning Centre going through vicissitudes, finally leaving Raman to lose both his aunt who does not approve of his proposal to marry

Daisy and his would-be wife. The story is parallel to the ancient Indian legend of King Shanthanu's love for Ganga. Like Ganga, Daisy begins to lay down conditions on which she would marry Raman. The action of the novel takes-place against the background of Malgudi. The plot is usual and the love-affair is dealt with half seriously and half humorously in the course of a perfect story having a beginning, a middle and an end.

The youngest of the major trio, Raja Rao, was born in Mysore on November 5, 1908 in an old and learned Brahmin family. When he was in the Aligarh Muslim University he met Professor Dickinson who encouraged him to study French and English literatures. He graduated from Madras University and at the age of twenty-one, in 1929, he sailed for France to do research on the mysticism of the West at Montpellier and Sorbone Universities under Professor Cazamian. Deeply influenced by sages like Pandit Taranath of the Tungabhadra Ashram and Sri Atmananda Guru of Trivandrum he saw that writing was his true vocation. Raja Rao is a novelist who constantly discusses the nationalist struggle and its revolutionary implications in terms of Hindu mythology, religion and culture.

Raja Rao's first novel *Kanthapura* (1938) is a most poetic novel dealing with the Gandhian Civil Disobedience Movement put up by the people of Kanthapura in the nineteen thirties. The story is narrated by the village grandmother in a series of happenings. Moorthy, a follower of Gandhi, advises people about "Swarajya," "Khaddar" and he also indoctrinates the Kanthapurans by putting new Gandhian wine into the age-old bottle of traditional Harikatha. This novel is discussed elaborately in Chapter 2 of this book.

The next novel *The Serpent and the Rope* (1960) (Sahitya Akademi Award, 1963) is the almost elaborately discussed novel. The scope of the novel is encyclopedic. The 'Serpent' and the 'Rope' are the symbols of "illusion" and "reality." Vedant philosophy is the subject of the novel. The story is of Ramaswami, a South Indian Brahmin, who, while doing research in history, in France, meets and marries Madeleine, a lecturer in history, but they soon drift apart as Ramaswami comes to know the difference between the Indian and Western conceptions of love, marriage and family after his meeting with a Cambridge-educated and wholly modern girl Savithri, who is yet Indian to the core. Finally, Madeleine, after the death of her two children, withdraws not only from her husband but also from the world and Ramaswami realises that his love for Savithri, not for his fulfilment in physical union, leads him to higher love, *i.e.*, union of the soul with God. The novel ends when he sets out for Travancore in search of ' "Him" to whom I have to go. Savithri, in this sense, plays a Guru to him before his joining the proper Guru in the end.

Raja Rao's next novel *The Cat and Shakespeare* (1965) deals with a few middle class families of Kerala during II World War. Pai and Nair are next door neighbours. Pai's wife is a practical minded woman. They have two children—Usha, a girl and Vithal, a boy. Pai falls in love with a young school mistress Shantha, who has a child by him. Shantha gives him her private money for the purchase of a house. Nair loses his son Shridhar who is supposed to marry Pai's daughter Usha. On the charge of bribery Shridhar is locked up in prison in spite of the High Court's release. He shifts elsewhere from Trivandrum. The cat plays a vital part ir. the incident at the office which was evidently meant as a practical joke against him. But the joke has a tragic consequence, for the office boss, Bhutalinga lyer, dies when the cat jumps on his head. The cat is brought as evidence in the court. The story is very thin indeed. About the novel Dr. M.K. Naik remarks: "The form of the novel is composite, a blend of the beast fable, the rogue story and the parable, and the dialogue frequently has an Upanishadic flavour."[7]

Comrade Kirillov (1976), the latest novel of Raja Rao, deals with the story of Padmanabham Iyer living in the West from 1928 to 1947, who has a son Kamal, by his Czech wife, Irene. The story is, in the main, narrated by lyer's friend R, whose relationship to Iyer is analogous to that between Kirillov and

Shatov in Dostoevsky's *The Possessed*. Being a communist rejecting Indian values on the surface but keeping conflict between the New and the Old deep within, lyer adopts an anti-"Quit India" stance during II World War and Irene dies in childbirth leaving Kamal behind. But it is seen from her diary that she had penetrated through Iyer's mask and seen his elemental love for India. She sees that when he touches Indian soil all his Western veneer will turn into European hatred. After the war Iyer disappears behind the communist iron curtain while Kamal joins his grandparents in India. Afterwards Kamal is at Kanyakumari with the help of R and for him India becomes identified with Eternal Virgin Parvati. Thus, in the novel orthodoxy and modernism, Gandhism and Communism, inner certitude and other frenzy are contradictory pulls to Iyer—and the novel shows that "holy Wedded Love" for an Indian with a European wife is impossible and an Indian's attempt for winning a fulfilled life outside the native land is foredoomed to failure. There are suggestions of the East-West theme in the picture of the Kirillov-Irene relationship. Thus as a writer of philosophical amplitude, Raja Rao has brought to the Indo-Anglian novel an epic vision, symbolic richness, lyrical fervour and above all an essential Indianness of style.

Muslim Novelists and their Works

Ahmad Ali, who became a Pakistani after partition, wrote *Twilight in Delhi* (1940) which is discussed in detail in Chapter 2 of this book. His second novel *Ocean of Night* (1964) deals with the decadent aristocracy of Lucknow Muslim society. In the novel Huma, the well-known courtesan of Lucknow, the mistress of Nawab Chhakkan, is left by the Nawab when he takes another prostitute as his mistress. Huma falls in love with a young lawyer but he finally cools down as his relation with her is a bit shameful. At last, the Nawab, in desperation, shoots Kesar Bai and himself. Indeed, leisurely Lucknow life is pictured in the novel.

Next we see Iqbalunnisa Hussain's *Purdah and Poligamy: Life in an Indian Muslim Household* (1944) depicting the picture of a traditional Muslim mercantile household. Again, Humayun Kabir in his *Men and Rivers* (1945) depicts the lives of the fisherman by the side of Padma river and the impact of the changing moods of the river upon these lives. Amir Ali's *Conflict* (1947), a political novel, is discussed in Chapter 3 of this book. His two later novels *Via Geneva* (1967) and *Assignment in Kashmir* (1973) are diplomatic novels. K.A. Abbas's various novels including film scripts appeared on the scene. His *Tomorrow Is Ours: A Novel of the India of Today* (1943) discussing several thematic causes like nationalism, leftism and denunciation of fascism and untouchability; and *Inquilab: A Novel of the Indian Revolution* (1955) dealing with the Indian Independence struggle of the twenties and thirties, are strong political novels discussed in Chapter 3 of this book.

Other Novelists

Dhan Gopal Mukherji (1890-1936), a novelist of jungle and rustic life, wrote *Kari, the Elephant* (1922); *Hari, the Jungle Lad* (1924); *My Brother's Face* (1926); *Gay-neck, the Story of a Pigeon* (1927); *The Chief of the Herd* (1929) and *Ghond the Hunter* (1929). Most of these novels deal with the animal world. But *Ghond the Hunter* is a travel book in which the boy Ghond is made to travel through Kashmir, Agra and Delhi so that the novelist may describe these places. The hero even spends a night in a Ladakh village and the novelist describes a landslide.

The period also produced the following novels: C.S. Rau's *The Confessions of a Bogus Patriot* (1923); J. Chinnadurai's *Sugirtha* (1929); Ram Narain's *Tigress of the Harem* (1930); H. Kaveribai's *Meenakshi's Memoirs*: A *Novel of Christian Life in South India* (1937); Shankar Ram's *The Love of Dust* (1938); D.F. Karakka's *Just Flesh* (1941); *There Lay the City* (1942) and *We Never Die* (1944), a political novel; C.N. Zutshi's *Motherland* (1944); a political novel; Purushottamdas Tricumdas's *Living Mask* (1947) and N.S. Phadke's *Leaves in the August Wind*

(1947) and *The Whirlwind* (1956) both are discussed in Chapter 2.

Indo-Anglian Novels (Independence and After)

Post Independence Indo-Anglian novelists carry over the social realism established earlier by Mulk Raj Anand, and retains the momentum the novel had gained during the age of Freedom Struggle. Contemporary Indo-Anglian novelists look at man in relation to society and as such, write novels on the themes of poverty; hunger; disease; misery of the poor; tradition and modernity; social evils and tensions; interchanging values of modern civilisation; crisis of character; East-West cultural contact, etc.

The earliest social and realistic novelist of the period is Bhabani Bhattacharya. who believes in the novel's having a social purpose and placing something before the reader and to whom art is that "it must teach, but unobtrusively, by its vivid interpretation of life. Art must preach, but only by virtue of its being a vehicle of truth."[8] We deal with his novels from the third chapter onwards.

Bhattacharya's renowned contemporary Manohar Malgonkar (1913-) is a realist believing in the entertainment value of art. In most of his novels male characters dominate the world where women seem just like instruments of masculine pleasure. A retired army officer, he came out with his first novel *Distant Drum* (1960). Through the character of pre-Independence Indian army officer Kiran the novel tries to analyse the mind of the Indian army at the most critical period of partition of India and Pakistan when riots were taking place and Hindus and Muslims were sharply divided on almost every issue. The next novel *Combat of Shadows* (1962) shows how the two shadows of 'desire' and 'aversion' are always active to take possession of the soul of man through the character of Henry Winton, the young British Manager of an Assam Tea Garden who is responsible for the deaths of an Indian Shikari and a

Eurasian who keeps an affair with his wife and who at last pays with his own life for these deaths.

The Princes (1963), a successful political novel, dealing with the merger of princely states and *A Bend in the Ganges* (1964), a political novel set against the background of partition are discussed in detail in Chapter 2. *Spy in Amber* (1971), is a spy thriller specifically written for film story.

The Devil's Wind (1972), Malgonkar's sixth novel which he calls Nana Saheb's story, is more the story of Nana Saheb, the last Peshwa, than of the mutiny of 1857, its historical background. This is the first perfect historical novel reflecting the Sepoy Mutiny of 1857 and projecting great historical figures as its characters. *Shalimar* (1978) is based on the story of the film "Shalimar" written by Krishna Shah, the director of the film and so it is not a novel proper. *Open Season* is the novelisation of the film script of the same name.

Khushwant Singh (1918-), a contemporary of Desani and writer of his own Sikh community, is a realistic novelist. He wrote in a hard and vigorous style employing colourful Punjabi expletives and terms of abuse. His first novel *Train to Pakistan* (1956) dealing with the impact of partition on Mano Majra, a small village on the Indo-Pakistan border, which is an epitome of India with Sikhs, Hindus and Muslims living in harmony until Independence and his second novel *I Shall Not Hear the Nightingale* (1959) dealing with a political theme are elaborately discussed in Chapter 2.

S. Menon Marath (1906-) is a realistic novelist of Kerala. All his novels are set against the soil of his native Kerala. His *Wound of Spring* (i960) dealing with a strong political theme is discussed in detail in Chapter 2 later; and his second novel *The Sale of an Island* (1968) is a social novel dealing with the conflict between Kumaran and the landlord, Sekhara Menon and ending with the eviction of all the tenants and the death of Kumaran.

Balchandra Rajan (1920-) is a critical realist. His novel *The*

Dark Dancer (1959) tells the story of the clash of cultures through the character of Krishnan, a South Indian Youth who is torn between his love for the British girl Cynthia and his loyalty to his wife Kamala, on his return from England to post-Partition India. His second novel *Too Long in the West* (1961) portrays Nalini, the heroine who faces the problem of choosing a husband through advertisement after her three years' stay at Columbia.

Like Rajan, an academic who lived too long in the West, Sudhin Nath Ghose (1899-1965) appears with his four novels namely *And Gazelles Leaping* (1949); *Cradle of the Clouds* (1951); *The Vermilion Boat* (1953) and *The Flame of the Forest* (1955) forming a tetralogy knit together by the protagonist narrator, about twenty years of whose life they cover. The tetralogy actually deals with the nameless hero's mind shaped by both his boyhood years in a traditional rural community and his youthful experiences in the city of Calcutta.

Next we see Govindas Vishnudas Desani's (1909-) *All About H. Hatterr* (1948) which is a humorous novel dealing with the seven incidents in the life of Mr. H. Hatterr, son of a European father and Malayan mother. It is a complex novel revealing social aspects of White, Eurasian and Indian characters. It depicts the hero's quest for understanding the meaning of life in a style blending Western and Indian narrative forms. M. Anantanarayan (1907-) wrote *The Silver Pilgrimage* (1961) with oriental form of narrative set in 16th century Ceylon and India. Depicting prince Jaysura's pilgrimage to Kashi, it discusses various manifestations of the divine. There is an overload of philosophy in the plot of the novel which is weak in content.

One of the prominent novelists of the sixties and seventies is Arun Joshi (1939-). He is a novelist handling the themes of alienation, the relation to self, the society around and humanity. His first novel *The Foreigner* (1968) deals with the theme of alienation of Sindi Oberoi from all humanity. Educated in the U.S.A. and England for 25 years and developing a philosophy of detachment in himself he loves an American girl and the love ends tragically both for the girl and for his bosom friend, Babu. The second novel *The Strange Case of Billy Biswas* (1971) is the story of a sophisticated young man leaving his native state for a tribal state in central India. He has been leaving with a girl named Bilasia. The tribal people accept him as a demigod. His happy life ends, when, during an attempt by his near relations to reclaim him, he is shot dead accidentally by a policeman. Thus an atmosphere of unreality is depicted in it.

Joshi's third novel *The Apprentice* (1974), a prolonged dramatic monologue in prose deals with Ratan Rathor describing how his father died, how he had to go hunting for a job and how at last he became a member of the urban elite. There is the revolting spectacle of hypocrisy, bribery, graft and drunkenness till at last Ratan gives all this up and becomes a shoeshiner on the stairway of a Delhi temple. *The Last Labyrinth* (1981) deals with the story of Som's misadventure with his dark and terrible love and it is a paradigm of the contemporary diseased world.

Chaman Nahal (1927-) is another recent novelist. His first novel *My True Face* (1973) deals with Kamal Kant's search for his wife Malati throughout Delhi and its outskirts, but having found her at the end he realises that their marriage is broken beyond repair. There is the element of realism in depicting many scenes in this novel, *Azadi* (1975), winning Sahitya Akademi award for 1977, gives an account of the migration of Lala Kanshi Ram, a Sialkot grain merchant and his family to India during the time of partition. The novel is fully discussed in Chapter 2.

Nahal's next novel *Into Another Dawn* (1977) deals with East-West encounter through the character of his hero, Ravi, a Hardwar Brahmin going to the U.S.A. for higher studies and falling in love with an American woman, the unhappy wife of a business executive and eloping with her, but finally, discovering his own terminal cancer, returns to Hardwar to die. *The Crown and the Loincloth* (1981) deals with the story of Shanti Nath's fourth son Sunil's Gandhian movement. It is discussed elaborately in Chapter 2. In *The English Queens* (1979) Nahal narrates the love story of Rekha, an army officer's daughter in a select colony, for a poor musician of the adjoining slum. The novel's plot moves uncertainly through realistic social satire, comic extravaganza and supernatural fantasy. Only the satire and the extravaganza are successfully worked out whereas the supernatural motif is crudely handled in this novel.

Women Novelists

Indian women novelists, like the women poets, have developed a style of their own in post-Independence fiction. Of all the women novelists Kamala Markandaya is the most appealing and outstanding novelist. Born in 1924 in South India she was educated casually and at intervals at Madras University, the intervals being spent travelling about India and Europe. The important themes in most of her novels are—East West encounter, women in different roles, etc. Her first novel *Nectar in a Sieve* (1954) is often compared to Pearl Buck's *Good Earth.* It recounts the touching tale of sorrow and misery of Rukmini, a farmer's wife in India who has the courage to triumph over disaster. The novel portrays love, hunger, lust, passion, ambition, sacrifice and death in modern Indian cities.

Markandaya's *Some Inner Fury* (1955) dealing with a political theme is discussed in detail in Chapter 2 of this book. The third novel *A Silence of Desire* (1960) deals with spiritual realities showing the end where it begins and shifting the main character from the female to the male. It depicts the clash between the Western oriented rationalism of Dandekar, who wants his wife Sarojini to get herself operated for a tumour and the traditional religious faith of Sarojini relying on the faith-healing of the Swami. In the fourth novel *Possession* (1963) the story is narrated by Anasuya and it is about a clash between Lady Caroline and a Swami for the "possession" of the soul of Valmiki, the rustic artist, who is lured to England by her, but later returns to his mentor.

Markandaya's fifth novel *A Handful of Rice* (1966) deals with the hard struggle of modern city life and its overall demoralisation. The novel narrates the story of Ravi, a farmer's son reaching a city and falling a victim to the machinations of petty culprits. He falls in love with Nalini, a handsome lass and marries her. She is a typical long-suffering Hindu wife and all her attempts to transform his life get foiled and thus the story shows failures in personal life and its struggle. Markandaya's sixth novel *The Coffer Dams* (1969) centres round the construction of a dam over a turbulent hilly river, the middle-aged British engineer Clinton and his young enthusiastic wife Helen and the situations made by the immates of the white quarters and the tribesman.

The next novel *The Nowhere Man* (1972) deals with the life of an Indian who settles down in London and who finds a kindred soul in Mrs. Pickering, a divorcee. But he is persecuted during the anti-immigrant wave of the sixties although he has some sympathetic white neighbours. He dies when a fanatic sets fire on his house. So the novel is of racial problem in England and it is a plea for human dignity and sanity. The next novel *Two Virgins* (1973) deals with the tale of Indian village life. It depicts the contrast between two sisters, Lalitha, the "child of grace," who yearns to become a "town miss" and Saroja, the "child of the soil" and the "country miss." The theme of the adolescent's loss of innocence is very depthly handled here. The latest but the longest and the most ambitious of all her novels is *The Golden Honeycomb* (1977) covering three generations of the princely family of Devapur. There are scenes of elaborate description like that of the Delhi Darbar of 1903 and the psychological workings of the minds of the characters in it. Along with scenes of local colour, there are incidents like Prince Rabi's affair with a slum girl in Bombay. The upshot is like a honeycomb from which the queen bee is missing.

Ruth Prawer Jhabvala (1927-) was born of Polish parents in Germany, though the family migrated to England in 1939. She was educated in London University from where she took her

Master's degree in English. She married an Indian architect and that gave her access to Indian society on terms radically different from those of contemporary writers,. She now lives in Delhi with her three daughters. A Jane Austen of India, she, indeed, is one of the loveliest and most urbane fiction writers. Her fictions deal with the traditional codes of conduct clashing with modern aspirations. Her eight novels, dealing with middle class Indian life especially in undivided Hindu families and ironic studies of the East and West encounter are put into two categories, the first of which comprises *To Whom She Will* (1955); *The Nature of Passion* (1956); *The Householder* (1960); and *Get Ready for Battle* (1962); and the second consists of—*Esmond in India* (1958); *A Backward Place* (1965); *A New Dominion* (1973) and *Heat and Dust* (1975).

To Whom She Will deals with a vivid social observation, social etiquette and social manners. A young man and woman enjoy the illusion of romantic love before accepting a separate arranged marriage each. *The Nature of Passion* depicts a successful, patriarchal businessman so attached to his youngest daughter that he is reluctant to get her married into a rich family, though the match will further his own business interests; but finally he succumbs to the pressure of his family. *The Householder,* a successful comedy of middle class Indian life deals with the story of a youth, newly married, who learns through trial and error the privileges and pains of becoming a grihastha. *Get Ready for Battle,* set against the background of the social atmosphere of the modern world, deals with the story of a businessman's becoming thwarted by his social worker type of wife from his desire for acquiring poor people's land by evicting them and his separation from her at the end.

The first novel of the second group *Esmond in India* depicts the marriage between a lazy, stupid but beautiful Indian girl and a snobbish, colonial-minded English expatriate that results in their separation. *A Backward Place* describes the struggles and sufferings of the English girl Judy, married to the Indian doctor, Bal. The novel depicts the clash of backgrounds, a middle-aged Hungarian beauty Elter keeping a number of Indian husbands and lovers, and Clarissa, another English woman devoted to Indian spiritualism. *A New Dominion* deals with the story of three European girls being caught in the toils of a fake Swami. The novel projects a European view of modern India.

The last of the second group *Heat and Dust* deals with the story of a young English girl in post-Independence India who finds herself unconsciously repeating, with inevitable variations, patterns of behaviour of her step-grandmother of the colonial days. The novel depicts the lives of two Englishmen in India. Heat and dust are the two things the European women do not like in India. Olivia, the wife of Douglas, Asst. Collector of Satipur also keeps "windows shut to keep out the heat and dust." But she elopes with the Nawab of Khatm and is one of the two heroines the novel has in its double mirror of time. Douglas got a divorce from Olivia and married Jessie. The narrator is Jessie's granddaughter narrating the story of her step-grandmother Olivia.

Nayantara Sahgal (1927-), an exponent of political novel, a daughter to Vijayalakshmi Pandit and niece to Jawaharlal Nehru, had been brought up in the midst of politics. Her fiction deals with politics and modern Indian woman's search for sexual freedom and self-realisation. Her five political novels—*A Time To Be Happy* (1958), *This Time of Morning* (1965), *Storm in Chandigarh* (1969), *The Day in Shadow* (1971), *A Situation in New Delhi* (1977) are discussed in detail in the second chapter of this book.

Anita Desai (1937-) is the youngest of the major Indo-Anglian women novelists. Anita Desai is a German on her mother's side and Bengali on her father's side. Her maiden novels put her in the front rank among the contemporary novelists. *Her Voices in the City* (1965), and *Cry, the Peacock* (1963) are much acclaimed novels. *Cry, the Peacock* deals with the married life of Maya with Gautama who is a middle-aged lawyer. *Voices in the City* deals with the alienated individuals in Nirode and his two sisters Monisha and Amla.

Bye-Bye Blackbird (1971) depicts the picture of an Indian living in London. Social and political realities and London and the British countryside are vividly and realistically depicted in this novel. England says good-bye to the black birds like Adit (who is homesick) and the black birds fly home (India). *Where Shall We Go This Summer* (1975) deals with the inner workings of the mind of her characters. Sita, married to Raman, cannot adjust her life with her in-laws and even with her children. When she finds herself pregnant again she gets panicky and does not want the birth of the child. She runs away to an island which is her childhood association. Finally, she returns to the city on her husband's persuasion since no miracles come to her. *Fire on the Mountain* (1977) is a beautiful haunting story of two old women and a convalescent girl in the hill town of Kasauli. *Clear Light of Day* (1980) deals with a theme of seeing the light in the mind of Vimala, the protagonist.

Another woman novelist Santha Rama Rau wrote two novels. *Remember the House* (1956) deals with the story of Bombay upper class society with its sophisticated ladies, drinking parties and princes. There is a picture of East-West encounter affecting young Indira's growth from adolescence to maturity which is another theme. *The Adventuress* (1970) depicts a young Philippino girl, stranded in post war Japan, her life in Manila and Shanghai. The novelist shows her insight into the character of Western men and women.

Nergis Dalal wrote the following novels: *Minari* (1967), portraying high class life at a hill station, with conventional characters in stock situations; *Two Sisters* (1973) depicting a realistic life of Bombay Parsee family and the love-affair between a Parsee girl and a Hindu boy; *The Inner Door* (1975) dealing with the theme of enforced sainthood as handled in Narayan's *The Guide; The Girls from Overseas* (1979) showing the treatment of East-West encounter.

Venu Chietale's *In Transit* (1950) portraying three generations of a Poona Brahmin joint family between the two world wars; Zeenuth Futehally's *Zohra* (1951) showing the lives of Muslim families of Hyderabad in the Gandhian age and Attia Hosain's *Sunlight On a Broken Column* (1951) depicting an aristocratic life in Pre-partition Lucknow are all political novels discussed fully in Chapter 2.

The following works of women novelists appeared during the sixties and seventies—Lotika Ghose's *White Dawns of Awakening* (1950); Mrinalini Sarabhai's *This Alone is True* (1952); Bani Ray's *Srilata and Sampa* (1953); Sally Athogia's *Gold in the Dust* (1966); Tapati Mukherjee's *Murder Needs a Staircase* (1962); and *Six Faces of Eve* (1963); Padmini Sengupta's *Red Hibiscus* (1962); Muriel Wasi's *Too High for Rivalry* (1967) portraying a fine school girl; Hilda Raj's *The House of Ramiah* (1967); Sita Ratnamal's *Beyond the Jungle* (1968); Meenakshi Puri's *Pay on the First* (1968); Veena Paintal's *Serenity in Storm* (1966) and *Midnight Woman* (1979); Raji Narasimhan's *The Heart of Standing is you cannot Fly* (1973) and *Forever Free* (1979) dealing with a young woman's search for fulfilment; Bharati Mukherjee's *Tiger's Daughter* (1973) and *Wife* (1976) depicting the frustration of a Bengali wife in New York; *Karmayogi* (1974) and *Compulsion* (1975) of Veena Nagpal dealing with vengeance; Jai Nimbkar's *Temporary Answers* (1974); Shanta Rameshwar Rao's *Children of God* (1976) with a Harijan woman as protagonist, Kamala Das's *Alphabet of Lust* (1976); Rama Mehta's *Inside the Haveli* (1977) dealing with the story of Rajasthan Purdah life, Sahitya Akademi award winner for 1979; Shouri Daniel's *The Salt Doll* (1977); Jyoti Jafa's *Nurjahan* (1978); Uma Vasudeva's *The Song of Anasuya* (1978) and Anita Kumar's *The Night of the Seven Dawns* (1979).

The following novelists of the post-Independence period have also produced fiction adding to the corpus of the Indo-Anglian novels. Anand Lall's *The House at Adampur* (1956) and *Seasons of Jupiter* (1958) depict base upper class life and the pursuit of pleasure followed by renunciation and returning back to the world respectively. M.V. Rama Sarma's *The Stream* (1956) and *Look Homeward* (1976) deal with East-West encounter with a hero going abroad for education. His *The Farewell Party* (1976) discussing the reverie of a professor on the day of his retirement, reflects educational scene in India. The same writer's *The Bliss of Life* (1979) deals with the life of Kshetrayya, the ancient Andhra saint poet. An Anglo-Indian, Ruskin Bond, wrote *The Room on the Roof* (1956), in which an Eurasian boy's reactions to colourful Indian scene is studied; *An Axe for the Rani* (1972), and *Love is a Sad Story* (1975). Jatindra Mohan Ganguli wrote—*When East and West Meet* (1961); *Two Mothers* (1964); *Fire on the Snows of Himalayas* (1965); *The Fisherman of Kerala* (1967) and *Bond of Blood* (1967) all deal with variety of scene and setting. Romen Basu also wrote—*A House Full of People* (1968); *A Gift of Love* (1974) and *Candles and Roses* (1978) and *Portrait on the Roof* (1980).

Of the post-Independence novels, mention may be made of the following: Dilip Kumar Roy's *The Upward Spiral* (1949), a philosophical novel; Hathi Singh's *Maura* (1951), a political novel; Aubrey Menen's *The Prevalence of Witches* (1955); S.V. Krishnaswami's *Kalyani's Husband* (1957); Victor Anant's *The Revolving Man* (1959), dealing with John Atma's position between the East and the West worlds; K.J. Shridharani's *Adventures of an Upside Down Tree* (1957); P.M. Nityananda's *The Long, Long Days* (1960); K.B. Vaid's *Steps in Darkness* (1962); Ved Mehta's *Delinquent Chacha* (1967); Nirmal Jacob's *Monsoon: A Story of Kerala* (1968); R.K. Laxman's *Sorry, No Room* (1969); Dilip Hiro's *A Triangular View* (1969) dealing with three Indian youths in Britain; B.K. Karanjia's *More of an Indian* (1970); Leslie de Noronha's *The Mango and the Tamarind Tree* (1970); Timeri Murari's *The Marriage* (1972); Reginald and Jamila Massey's *The Immigrants* (1973); Sasthi Brata's *She and He* (1973); Saros Cowasjee's *Goodbye to Elsa* (1975); A. Bhaskar Rao's *The Secret* (1978); S.S. Dhami's *Maluka* (1978); K.M.

Trishanku's *Onion Peel* (1973), a story of a sexual orgy; Buny Reuben's *You, I and He* (1973), etc.

Mention may also be made of the following novels like Raj Gill's *The Rape* (1974), a political novel, *The Golden Dawn* (1974) and *The Infidel* (1979); D.R. Manekar's *No, My Son, Never* (1974); Nishi Khanolkar's *Dwasuparna* (1976); B.S. Gidwani's *The Sword of Tipu Sultan* (1976); Rohit Handa's *Comrade Sahib* (1977); a study of the Naxalite movement; H.S. Gill's *Ashes and Petals* (1977); Rattan Mann's *Silence with the Storm* (1978) and *Holier Than Thou* (1978); Kasthuri Srinivasan's *A Handful of Earth* (1973) and *Service with a Smile;* Vikram Kapur's *The Traumatic Bite* (1978); a sex dominated novel; Shiv K. Kumar's *The Bone's Prayer* (1979), dealing with sexual betrayal and *Trapped* (1979), the recent publication of Narendrapal Singh.

Indian born Salman Rushdie's oversize political novel, *Midnight's Children* (1981), published in U.K. and U.S.A., deals with the history of India from pre-Independence to the time of Emergency (1975-77). The novel is fully discussed in chapter 2 of this book. S.P. Mani's short novel *In Person* (1976) deals with the theme of God-man. Shashi Deshpande's *The Dark Holds No Terrors* (1980) is a remarkable novel. Ahmed M. Akhtar (Ahmad Mohiuddin)'s *The Blood Red Bangles* (1976) and *The Monument* (1977), the former recalls life in the early 1920's while the latter takes us back to the "Sepoy Mutiny" of 1857. Sharf Mukaddam's *When Freedom Came* (n.d.) is the story of extremist or communist politics. Deepchand C. Becharry's *That Others Might Live* (1976); Shyam Dave's *The Kumbh Docket* (1972); S. Gopalan's *Jackal Farm* (1974); K.D. Khosla's *Never the Twain* (1981); Akhileswar Jha's *The Janapath Kiss* (n.d.); are all realistic novels of the time. Gopalan's *Tryst with Destiny* (1981) deals with the story of Gandhian struggle, Netaji's I.N.A. and the coming of freedom followed by Gandhi's martyrdom.

In justification of the above general perspective and also of the following chapter, we have to briefly summarise our position thus:

In an attempt to analyse and discuss the art of Indian political fiction with special reference to Bhabani Bhattacharya, a political and realistic novelist of the social ferment, a glimpse of the history of the Indo-Anglian fiction is appropriate. As the Indo-Anglian writer writes primarily from what he has known as literature and primarily for the Indian reader with a similar literary awareness, he may be viewed only in the perspective of, firstly, the literature in his own language and secondly, in that of other Indo-Anglian writers. A brief study of the panoramic scene of the growth of the Indo-Anglian fiction gives us an idea of how political and social novels grew under the motivation of political protests and social reforms in the course of history. Indeed, an Indo-Anglian novel is to be read only in this context and not of that which the European reader is used to.

A general survey of the Indo-Anglian fiction affords us the opportunity to detect the place of political novels, their dominant themes and the circumstances under which they have been growing up at the turns and twists of the history of the present century. The study of the rise and development of Indo-Anglian fiction shows the position of Bhabani Bhattacharya's novel expressing socio-political, economic and philosophico-cultural ideas.

The brief study of the Indo-Anglian novels in this chapter gives only a hint of the ideas to be discussed in the later chapter. This general survey of the Indo-Anglian fiction is only an attempt at creating a context for the discussion of the kind of political novel that Bhattacharya wrote.

REFERENCES

1. V.K. Gokak, *English in India: Its Present and Future.* Bombay: 1964, 161.
2. Mulk Raj Anand, *The King Emperor's English.* Bombay, 3.
3. P.P. Mehta, *Indo-Anglian Fiction: An Assessment* (Bareilly: Prakash Book Depot, 1979), 185.
4. Mehta 235.
5. "The Technique of R.K. Narayan's *Guide,*" *The Western Humanities Review,* Vol. XV, No. 4, Autumn, 1961.

6. H.M. Williams, *Indo-Anglian Literature (1800-1970): A Survey* (Delhi: Orient Longman Ltd., 1976), 61.
7. M.K. Naik, *A History of Indian English Literature*, (New Delhi: Sahitya Akademi, 1982), 172.
8. Bhabani Bhattacharya, "Literature and Social Reality," *The Aryan Path*, XXVI, No. 9, Sept. 1955.

2

Definition and Interpretation of Political Novel and Its Scope in Indian Writing in English and Dominant Themes of Indian Political Novels

1. Various Definitions of Political Novel

Of the conventional categories of the novel such as: the historical, picaresque, and psychological, novel of manners, science fiction, mystery novels, thrillers, political fiction, etc., the last category, *i.e.*, "political fiction" has not so far been defined consciously. This sub-genre "political fiction" or "political novel" has remained somewhat vague and amorphous even in the standard studies by such authorities as Irving Howe, Joseph L. Blotner and H.A.L. Fisher. Although some critics have tried to define the term 'political novel' as novel or fiction dealing with political ideology or, at any rate, the novel in which political events are acting as a backdrop against which literary characters are developed, yet the problem of defining the term has not been dealt with in any definitive way as in the case of the other sub-genres of prose fiction.

Perhaps, the lurking fear about the wedding of politics to literary creation, strange bed fellows, is the cause of the reluctance of critics to give a sharper definition. However, in spite of the fact that the very nature of this particular category of novel—its proper subject matter, its scope, its form—remains open to question, many acceptable though not precise or concise, definitions have become established so far.

Let us consider some of the attempts made to define the political novel. Morris E. Speare, in his endeavour to define precisely the political novel as a genre, describes it as:

> "a work of fiction which leans rather to "ideas" than to "emotions"—where the main purpose of the writer is party-propaganda, public reform or exposition of the lives of personages who maintain Government or of forces which constitute Government."[1]

H.A.L. Fisher seeks to give a broader definition:

> "The political novel concerns itself with men and women engaged in contemporary political life and discussing contemporary political ideas."[2]

To Joseph L. Blotner, "a political novel is a book which directly describes, interprets or analyses political phenomena;"[3] whereas Irving Howe remarks that "by a political novel I mean a novel in which political ideas play a dominant role or in which the political milieu is the dominant setting."[4]

Considering and comparing the above definitions Dr. M.K. Naik comes to the conclusion that the term "political novel" may denote either (a) "a piece of fiction devoted to a presentation of political ideas," or (b) "a species of fiction in which action, characters and setting are all firmly grounded in politics."[5] Disraeli's "young England' trilogy—*Coningsby, Sybil* and *Tancred,* is the finest example where both these types are combined in British fiction.

Analysing these several definitions by various eminent authorities we may conclude that the term "political novel" signifies a novel which, directly or indirectly, expresses and indicates certain ideological preferences or describes and analyses existing political conditions.

But Mahadev L. Apte strongly pleads that a political novel is quite different from a novel which includes politics in one form or another. According to him, any novel containing descriptions of political actions, events, ideologies, or whatever, is not necessarily a political novel. "The essential ingredients of a political novel include all of the following:

(1) The plot, if any, should be based on, or should include extensive political events;

(2) The principal characters in the novel should be directly involved with political activities in various capacities or should themselves play some political roles; alternatively, the consequences of any political event should directly affect the lives of the principal characters;

(3) The actions of the various characters in the novel should be the direct result of, and be consistent with, their personalities, which should be so depicted as to suggest strong influences of various political ideologies;

(4) If political events are used as a background for a variety of non-political actions and events, such background should be used throughout the novel either to support or to contrast the actions and events; furthermore, it should not be superseded by sociological or economic elements.

In short, the characters, the interaction between them, the events, all should be interwoven in a political milieu; political phenomena should be directly described, interpreted or analysed, and yet should be an integral part of the novel."[6]

An observation of these several definitions and established theories about "political novel" of various authorities and critics shows that a novel, if it is to be a political novel, should, at least, deal with a political ideology or should have a political setting against which fictional characters are seen to develop. Over and above these requirements, it may also be added that in a segmented society like India, where different linguistic, cultural and ethnic groups maintain autonomous status, novels describing their inter-relationships shall also be considered as political novels.

There may be two broad categories of political novels—ideologically oriented and non-ideological. The ideologically oriented group consists of those novels which have been written to propagate certain "Specific" political ideas, with a view to using them as vehicle of political propaganda. The characters are mainly used as instruments of ideological goals. In these novels the novelists interpret the political events on the basis of their own value orientations; they do not depict political reality, objectively; they distort it to reinforce their propagandistic goals. On the other hand, the non-ideological novelists are solely concerned with the depiction of political conditions and do not aim to propagate any specific political values. Their works have greater artistic objectivity. If there are expressions of certain political values in their novel, they can be attributed to their personal political orientations, rather than to this desire to propagandise.

There also arises the difficulty in distinguishing between political and historical novels. Even if the novel is written about contemporary political events or about current political personalities, it may come under the label "historical" because political events and personalities become part of history. One solution to this problem is the position of the author because he who writes about political events during his lifetime seems to consider his novel more political than historical. Another difference lies in the interpretation. A political novelist's interpretation of political events during his lifetime can be considered predictive, though particular projections may or may not come true. On the other hand, the historical novelist's interpretation is more likely to be retrospection or justification of events that have taken place.

On another plane of our discussion, it is rather difficult to define a political novel. It is too narrow and mechanistic to interpret a political novel as one portraying a political movement or depicting political condition, for most social problems have political dimensions. On this point V.N. Rao rightly remarks:

> "On the one hand, a novel about a social evil like untouchability becomes inevitably political in the context of Gandhiji's movement to eradicate untouchability. On the other hand, there are novels that have used a political movement only as a means of projecting the personal situation of the characters. Moreover, there are novels with no significant reference to any political situation but which nevertheless have a strong political message."[7]

2. Scope of Political Novel in Indian Writing in English

The scope of 'political novel' in Indian writing in English is very wide and large. It covers all the political problems and social problems in the history of Indian society because in it (history) political change is the most important change to which other changes become subordinate. It is difficult to distinguish between social problems and political problems since every social problem acquires a political dimension, pointing towards an all-encompassing political solution. In the history of Indo-Anglian novel the period before Independence was such a time when the prevailing concerns of political change were the most important and a study of political novel after Independence, therefore, first focuses our attention on the social novel before Independence.

The content of Indian novel changed considerably with the 1857 Rebellion caused by the rise of nationalism, fostered by British social and economic exploitation, and the subsequent assumption of rule by the British monarchy. In short, politics had now been included as a staple in the content of Indo-Anglian novel. Politics, political issues and polemics became the pre-occupation of the Indian novelists with the increase in nationalist activities during the thirties and forties. Indian aspiration for freedom and Independence from Britain gave birth to two categories of novels. To the first category belonged the works of those novelists who favoured non-violence and whose outlook could be called Gandhian. The second category consisted of the works of those novelists with Marxist and terrorist sympathies who wanted to expel the British by any means whatsoever, usually violent in nature. Only the means was significantly different while the end for both groups was essentially the same.

The seed time of Indian Independence was the decade of the 1930's, packed with the following remarkable events: the Gandhian salt satyagraha movements of 1930 and 1932, the three Round Table Conferences, the passing of the Government of India Act, 1935, the introduction of Provincial Autonomy in 1937, the Gandhian movement for Harijan Uplift and Basic Education, the organisation of Marxist parties of diverse hues, the involvement in war in 1939, the schism in the Congress leading to the expulsion of S.C. Bose and his eventual escape to Germany and Japan. These events deeply coloured the Indian psyche and, together with climactic events of the next decade, found expression in numerous literary works.

A perplexing reality was shown in the Post-Independence novels because the Marxists continued to write much in the same vein as their pre-Independence works whereas the Gandhians, disillusioned with partition, the Mahatma's assassination and the social and political turmoil in India, came to withdraw from their former political theme and turned to themes focused on personal and social themes. Examples are: R.K. Narayan's *The Guide*; Raja Rao's *The Serpent and the Rope* and *The Cat and Shakespeare*; B. Bhattacharya's *Music for Mohini, He Who Rides a Tiger*; B. Rajan's *Too Long in the West*; Arun Joshi's *The Foreigner* and *The Apprentice*; Chaman Nahal's *My True Face*; Kamala Markandaya's *Nectar in a Sieve*; R.P. Jhabvala's *To Whom She Will*; Anita Desai's *Cry, the Peacock*, etc. These writers turned to interpersonal relationships and spiritual problems for their themes. But the notable events of the sixties and early seventies — the 1962 border dispute with China, the 1965 Pakistani War, the emergence of the "Naxalites" or the pro-Peking Marxists and the 1971 Bangla Desh War (most of these involved armed conflict) brought back political fervour to fiction.

A new, more critical view of history and politics was bound to emerge.

The political novel has flourished in Indo-Anglian literature. But a political novel must preserve the integrity of its fictional values for its artistic success by a skilful handling of fictional elements—like the presentation of political ideas or ideologies or setting, action and characters. So long as this fictional law is observed by the Indo-Anglian novelists there will be a stream of artistically successful political novels in Indo-Anglian fiction, for the socio-political issues, looming in the still fresh memory of the struggle for freedom, may be seen to define the consciousness of the Indian writer.

3. Dominant Themes in Indian Political Novels

We have to analyse the influence of the political motif on the thematic construct of many political novels. For the sake of convenience in our analysis of the political novels and their dominant themes we may classify them according to their thematic similarities into the following groups:

(1) Early political novels based on armed rebellion against British rule;

(2) Political novels based on Gandhian ideology;

(3) Political novels based on the partition riots;

(4) Political novels based on the Post-Independence Political themes/issues.

Many of the novels falling into these groups had already been discussed in Chapter 1, but we attempt below a brief analysis of each group in another perspective, that of the evolution of the political consciousness itself.

1. Early Political Novels based on Armed Rebellion

We have already seen how the political theme is present in the earliest fictional works in Indo-Anglian literature, *viz.*, K.C. Dutt's *A Journal of Fortyeight Hours of the Year 1945* and S.C. Dutt's *Republic of Orissa : Anals from the Pages of the Twentieth Century*. Both have strong political themes based on armed rebellion by nationalists. The first was published on 6 June 1835 in "The Calcutta Literary Gazettee." It is significant that this novel by an Indian was produced before the acceptance of English Education by the Government of India. This novel depicts an imaginary unsuccessful uprising and revolt of the middle and upper-class English educated Indian people against the British rule a hundred and ten years later in 1945. Although this novel is like a tale rather than a proper political novel since the political colouring in it is largely an aid to fantasy alone, it depicts the beginning of Indian fiction in the political genre with a familiar theme: the national struggle against foreign rule.

The second novel depicts an imaginary British defeat leading to the establishment of a democratic republic in Orissa. Both novels are futuristic fantasies and are set in the 20th century. In spite of its being a fantasy, this 2nd novel has a technique more satisfactory than the first one and a plot founded on logical coherence. But the nationalist theme is equalled with personal vendetta.

The same theme of armed rebellion is dealt with in S.C. Dutt's *The Young Zamindar.* This novel reflects the sporadic armed revolts of the Indian Muslims and Hindus against the British authority and their suppression of the revolt in Orissa. A novel reflecting the Indian Mutiny of 1857 is the same author's *Shunkur: A Tale of Indian Mutiny of 1857.* The novel shows the mutiny in the manner of mingling history with fiction. Deprivation of the Indian upper class of their power and position and the cruelty of the British officials towards Indians are given as the cause of the outbreak of the mutiny. The prevailing tone is one of nationalism.

The next novel reflecting the colonial struggle of the time in the context of political formation of India League in 1857, Indian Association in 1876 and Indian National Congress in 1885 is S.K. Ghosh's *The Prince of Destiny: The New Krishna.* In this novel many contemporary problems, including the political independence, are woven together and it presents an enlightened Rajput prince combining in him the best in the East and the West. This novel, shows religion dominating Indian politics of those days. About the literary and fictional quality of the novel Bhupal Singh remarks:

> "In style and subject matter, and in a variety of its scenes and vividness of its descriptions, the book is above the ordinary."[8]

With an interesting plot and characters, all more idealistic than realistic, the novel attempts to present India's destiny in the background of colonialism.

One more novel based on Indian insurgency and armed rebellion and akin to *The Prince of Destiny* is S.M. Mitra's *Hindupore*. This novel deals with the right to political opinion and it parodies British rulers and communal leaders. It begins with all ideal friendly relation between the Indians and the British. But, later on, the British arrogance and their brutalities towards Indians provoke insurgency. The repressive measures of the government, the arrogance and the high-handedness of the British rulers are shown to be responsible for the Indian insurgency and agitation.

R. Tagore's *The Home and the World* is also a political novel set against the revolutionary background of 1905 Bengal chocked with the war-cries of "Swadeshi" and "Bandemataram." The story of the novel depicts the autobiographical sketches of three principal characters Nikhil, his wife Bimala and Sandip, his friend. Bimala, who has lived a sheltered life of a Hindu wife, suddenly hears the call of the outside world and thus she is torn between the pull of the "home" and the pull of the "world." In fact, this novel is strongly ideological because of the implications of the critical debate between Gandhism and terrorist politics.

Tagore's *Gora* is also a patriotic and political novel voicing the aspirations of the resurgent India. The social theme of the novel has a political undercurrent. The novel really reflects the patriotic zeal of Gora, the central character. It projects the all important political question: the conflict of ideals and aspiration between the East and the West. The weight of Tagore's own philosophy and poetic personality imparts special significance to these novels shown above. Both these novels were translated into English not long after their publications in Bengali, but since Tagore influenced all India, his novels could not be left out of our view.

2. Political Novels based on Gandhian Ideology

It is seen that the growth of the freedom movement intimately parallels the rise of the Indo-Anglian novels. In this context A.V. Krishna Rao's remark is worth close attention:

> "Almost all the Indo-Anglian novels have one or more of the following nuclear ideas predominant in them: the Evil of partition; the cult of 'Quit India;' and the Gandhian Myth.... It is significant that the image of Gandhi is present in all the three types of novels though the details and emphasis may vary."[9]

Describing Gandhi's role in the political and moral awakening of the masses N. Radhakrishnan aptly observes:

> "Gandhi's appeal to the rise in revolt was not directed to the new urban society but to the peasants who lived in India's 700,000 villages. He aimed at a happy marriage between politics and ethics, he faced each morning's issues in the light of eternal universal values."[10]

Indian writers inspired by the political ethics of Mahatma Gandhi played a part not less in importance than that of the frontline freedom fighters in arousing the national spirit in the people and in inspiring them with the zeal for freedom struggle. Many writers were active participants of the Gandhian programmes of freedom struggle. Thus Gandhi was the imitator of the overwhelming freedom struggle on which post-Independence political novels were based.

The impact of Gandhi on Indo-Anglian novel is beautifully summed up by Krishna Kripalani in the following words:

> "Gandhi's impact on Indian writers was direct and widespread. Apart from its political repercussions, it was both moral and intellectual and at once inhibitive and liberating. Gandhi stripped urban life and 'elegance' of their pretensions and culture without conscience were worthless. He transfigured the image of India and turned national idealism from its futile adulation of the past to face the reality of India as she was poor, starving and helpless, but with an untapped potential of unlimited possibilities.... His own employment of a simple and direct style, compact and incisive, shorn of all superfluities, both in English and his mother tongue Gujarati, was a very healthy corrective to the natural tendency of flamboyance in Indian writing."[11]

Thus with the impact of Gandhiji the Indian writers changed their high flown literary style of romanticism to realism. Observing the place of Gandhi and his influence on Indo-Anglian writing Dr. Minakshi Mukherjee rightly sums up:

> "No discussion of Indo-Anglian fiction dealing with the Independence movement would be complete without an assessment of the function of Mahatma Gandhi in these novels. The most potent force behind the whole movement, the Mahatma is a recurring presence in these novels and he is used in different ways to suit the design of each writer. He has been treated variously as an idea, a myth, a symbol, tangible reality and a benevolent human being. In a few novel he appears in person, in most others he is an invisible presence."[12]

Gandhi's influence on the Indians has been so profound that it has become impossible not to reflect his image and ideology in any of the novels dealing with the Independence movement. We may divide the novels in which Gandhi and his ideology is a recurring presence into four groups as under:

(1) Novels presenting Gandhi as a character; as in Narayan's *Waiting for the Mahatma*, K. Nagarajan's *Chronicles of Kedaram*, Anand's *Untouchable* and *The Sword and the Sickle*, etc.

(2) Novels in which Gandhi is represented by idealised characters like *Kanthapura* by R. Rao and *Kandan, the Patriot* by K.S. Venkataramani.

(3) Novels presenting Gandhi's followers, like, R.K. Narayan's *Vendor of Sweets* and Nayantara Sahgal's *A Time to be Happy*.

(4) Novels presenting Gandhian ideals, like B. Bhattacharya's *Shadow from Ladakh*.

These novels are discussed briefly in this chapter along with other novels of thematic similarity.

Venkataramani's *Murugan, the Tiller* and *Kandan, the Patriot* are two of the first Indo-Anglian novels dealing with the nationalistic revolution and freedom movement under the leadership of Gandhi. The first deals with the Gandhian ideal of rural reconstruction as a step towards winning freedom. It explores and applauds the Gandhian Satyagraha and overtly calls the Indians to work for freedom and regeneration as a nation. The central character Ramu plays the role of an ideal man with the aim of reconstructing Indian village where none slaved for another, an aim close to the Gandhian dream of "Going back to the village." Since the novel has the nationalist theme as its backbone we can treat it as a political novel although the national struggle for freedom is not reflected by it in a straightforward way.

The second novel deals with the freedom movement under the Gandhian politics. It is the story of Kandan's resignation "from the Indian Civil Service to plunge into the freedom struggle and his final succumbing to a police bullet. Here Gandhi is represented by idealised character, Kandan and the novelist shows Gandhi's presence in every village to lead the people. So Kandan says to Rajeswari Bai, a woman freedom fighter, that men like Gandhiji should be in every cottage working for its renovation.

Prof. P.P. Mehta criticises the novel as under:

> "The story is full of long patriotic speeches; the plot is unrealistic and the narration is not artistic. So the characters become mere dummies without life."[13]

But supporting the artistic and political quality of the novel and the skill of the novelist. G.P. Sarma fittingly remarks:

> "K.S. Venkataramani is the first really successful novelist in whose writing propaganda and artistic skill attained a happy, harmonious combination in the history of Indo-Anglian fiction."[14]

In spite of all vagueness and misgivings of the plot and characters it is a fact that Kandan is influenced by Gandhi in his view about "Swaraj." We should remember that Kandan, the patriot, was dedicated to "the unknown volunteer in India's fight for freedom."

Dhan Gopal Mukerjee's *My Brother's Face* is a novel dealing with the violent freedom struggle. The novelist describes the philosophical background of India and the narrator's American return brother as a child, as a school boy and as a youth. This brother, nourished on the Hindu religion, learnt Muslim stories and Christianity. While the leader of the freedom movement died of a police bullet this brother became the leader. He escaped from the hands of the C.I.D. and met with Mahatma Gandhi and learnt from him the value and idea of non-violence and non-co-operation, the real ways to fight with the British. Afterwards he became a follower of Gandhi. The spirit of freedom permeating through the novel makes it a political novel.

Not all political novels are good. For example, A Subramanyam's *Indira Devi*: *A Romance of Modern Political India* is neither a political novel nor a romance in the proper sense because all those reflections of the contemporary political scenes are too superficial to conform to the idea of the sub-title. Although the novel includes the national movement for abolition of caste system, Hindu Muslim disunity, development of a liberal society, etc., it remains a contrived love-story reflecting the adverse effect of a hurried attempt to reform the caste system and religious intolerance—a prevalent idea among the nationalists of South India.

Frieda H. Das's *Into the Sun* is a novel showing the impact of the Congress movement that changes the Indian social life. Reflecting the selfless voluntary services of Congress workers like Krishna, Rama Devi and Rukmini and their nationalistic leaning, firm resolutions and patience to fight for the improvement of the lot of the untouchables the novel portrays—the changing social order under the nationalistic ideal of the Congress party of India.

Anand's *Untouchable* deals indirectly with an aspect of Gandhian struggle for freedom in the thirties. The novel reflects Gandhi's tireless efforts for Harijan upliftment and his appearance and his public speech against the callous attitude of the British Government with their "divide and rule policy" and proposal for giving separate electorate in the council to the low and depressed classes under the new constitution.

Serving the classical three unities Anand describes a single day's events in the life of one 18 years old untouchable boy Bakha, son of Lakha, the Jamadar of sweepers of the town and cantonment. He is awakened by his father to clean the public latrines. While he is walking along enjoying the sights of the town a man touches him. But he is beaten down for defiling the man which is really the man's own fault. At the moment to the surprise of this boy a Muslim comes to his rescue. Then cursing his lot he reaches the temple where to his dismay he sees the Brahmin priest trying to molest his sister Sohini, a sweeper in that temple. He foils the attempt but the frustrated priest escapes into the crowd shouting that he has been polluted. After performing his duties he approaches to certain houses for food. But he realises that there is no food for the scavengers like him when there is enough for the "holy man" walking with the "readymade" blessings of God. Really for the essential services rendered by him he gets nothing but the sheer callousness of the beneficiaries.

In the afternoon Bakha hears of a meeting organised to be addressed by Mahatma Gandhi. Being freedom hungry, he is charmed by the word "Mahatma" and rushes to the Mahatma. In their way to the meeting ground the people take a short cut way by damaging the beautiful garden flowers and jumping over the fence. This symbolises destruction of the old civilisation making room for the new, represented by Gandhi. Bakha arrives at a crowded corner of the meeting ground where he hears people talking of Gandhi as a *legend*, a *tradition* and an *oracle* and of his courage and bravery as a bulletproof, swordproof and fireproof Mahatma who is able to overthrow the British Government as well as the whole world.

Meanwhile Gandhi appears at the scene and starts his speech on the topic of untouchability against the background of the contemporary Indian politics in which the Indians, on their seeking for freedom from foreign yoke, trample underfoot millions of human beings. Prof. G.P. Sarma gives a fitting remark on the theme of the novel thus:

> "The novel thus deals with the Hindu social problem of untouchability against the political background of the time, depicting at the same time people's faith in Gandhi as their leader in the national movement and his magnetic influence on the people."[15]

Bakha believes in Gandhi's power and capacity of removing all their present miseries. The novel ends with his contemplation on the three possibilities for his redemption—conversion to Christianity, abolition of untouchability and introduction of flush latrines. Thus, the novel projects Gandhi as a character championing the cause of the oppressed.

Anand's *Coolie* deals with the theme of social and economic exploitation of the poor class by the rich class under political background. It depicts the oppression of a peasant boy by the society. In the story a peasant boy is presented to be leaving his village home to become a domestic servant; to pass later on to a factory in one of India's cities; to become a worker in a Bombay cotton industry and finally to become a rickshaw puller along the steep hill of Simla to die of consumption.

Thus the novel depicts the injustice and oppression done by the rich to the poor; by the bourgeoisie to the proletariat, which are nothing but the outcome of a politically embroiled society. Really, this novel showing the exploitation of the coolies like Munoo (Mundu) by the forces of industrialism, capitalism, communism and colonialism, is a strong political novel grounded on the colonial society of India.

K.S. Nagarajan's *Athawar House* is a novel depicting the events of 15 years from 1919 to 1935 in a Marathi Brahmin family. Through this family story the novelist reveals the influence of the national movement under Gandhi on the town and the family. The history of freedom struggle provides three divisions of the novel:

Part I starts with the passing of the Rowlatt Bill in 1919 and ends with the all India hartal and mass arrest subsequent to the prince of Wales's landing at Bombay in 1921.

Part II starts with the Kanpur session of the Congress and ends with the acceptance of the constitution as drafted by the Motilal Nehru convention by the Calcutta Congress session in 1928.

Part III begins in 1929 with the terrorists' throwing bomb at the Delhi Assembly; the Viceroy's declaration of India's Dominion Status, and the Lahore Congress session's declaration of complete independence as its goal. It ends with the withdrawal of the Civil Disobedience Movement by the Congress in 1934.

In fact, with an emotional integration of the people of various regions of the country the novelist brings the idea of national integration and this leads to the political awakening of the people for the freedom of the nation.

Raja Rao's *Kanthapura* depicts the national struggle of the Gandhian era. It is a picture of the impact of the Gandhian ideology of the non-violent non-co-operation of an obscure village in South India during the 1930's. The small community of Kanthapura is shaken by the whirlwind of the Gandhian revolution. The Kanthapurians have been indoctrinated with the village Gandhi, young Moorthy's putting the new Gandhian wine into the age-old bottle of Harikatha (narrative of God based on ancient legend). Moorthy, who knows that the master-key to the Indian rustic mind is religion, makes the Kanthapurians convince of the ideology of the Mahatma who is like an avatar in the Hindu tradition and makes them plunge full-heartedly into the freedom struggle. This effort of the villagers under the leadership of Moorthy finally results to the wiping of both men and mosquitoes out of the village. In this context Dr. M.K. Naik remarks:

> "*Kanthapura* is, thus, a highly successful attempt to probe the depths to which the nationalistic uprising penetrated, the new patriotic upsurge fusing completely with the traditional religious faith and in the process rediscovering the Indian soul."[16]

The story depicts all the various aspects of the freedom struggle of the time which no novel till 1939 has depicted. It shows all the remarkable political events like Gandhi's *Dandi-March* to inaugurate the Civil Disobedience Movement in 1930 with the launching of Satyagraha by the villagers as response to this movement and their observance of non-cooperation by not paying taxes, formation of village Congress Committee loaded with constructive programmes—including Nehru's social programmes, Gandhi's decision to attend the Second Round Table Conference and nationwide influence for political emancipation, etc. Besides, social programmes of the Congress like the abolition of untouchability, propagandistic demonstration against drinking, attention on spinning, Satyagraha and fast by Gandhi's followers and police atrocities on the Congress

Gandhian volunteers are realistically portrayed as things combined together to win political and moral freedom. Here Gandhi is the driving force and is represented by the idealised character of Moorthy.

Ahmed Ali's *Twilight in Delhi* is also a novel set against the political background of the first two decades of this century. Although the political nationalist spirit breathed by the novel does not belong to any recognised phase of Indian freedom struggle, it is a strong political feeling of the whole of Muslim community at a particular period of our history. Dipping down deep in the nostalgia of the faded glories of the past and consequently growing into a rage Mr. Nihal, the central character of the novel, thinks of a free country and for which he might have joined the new political movement for freedom. The various political events like seditious revolutionary activities, the Home Rule and the Non-Cooperation Movements and the terrorists activities following the wake of national resurgence constitute the background against which develops this novel.

Anand's *The Sword and the Sickle* is also a novel where Gandhi appears as an apostle of non-violence. He is introduced only in one scene where a dialogue takes place between him and Lalu, the revolutionary dreaming of Marxist Utopia in India. Gandhi explains the doctrine of non-violence to Lalu. Though Gandhi fails to convince Lalu, Gandhi's influence over the illiterate peasants and the downtrodden and their faith in Gandhi dominate the novel. Thus plotting Lalu's meeting with Gandhi who impresses Lalu with his speech and advice of casting out fear in the freedom struggle the novel can come to the ambit of political novel.

Tomorrow Is Ours by K.A. Abbas is also a novel dealing with the story of the national struggle for Independence in Bengal in the pre-II world war period. The novel shows the career of an educated Indian dancing girl Parvati, her enthusiasm for political freedom and emancipation of women, and the superiority of Indian culture and the Indian way of life in a plot, gripping full of suspense. The novelist strikes at the international political scene struck at and disturbed by II World War and the Indian people's reaction to it. While Europe is fighting in a life and death struggle, India is progressing and hoping, "Tomorrow is Ours." Thus the novel deserves a place among political novels especially for depicting this Indian reaction to the then world situation.

Abbas's second novel *Defeat for Death* narrating three different stories—one about a child, another about an old man, and the third about a city, all distinct from one another, occurring at three different parts of the world and dealing with the same theme of oppression by the imperialists, defies classification.

The first two stories depict two events—the besiege of Stalingrade by Germany in 1942 and a negro boy's mental turmoil under the tyrannical grip of the imperialist race in two different parts of the globe. Parallel to this story the third story reveals an old man of seventy undergoing a fast at another part of this globe. The old man is identified with Gandhi in his fast in jail in 1942. Hearing the old man's success in his twenty-one day long fast the boy in the hospital becomes hopeful and optimistic about life. He is told about the invincible courage of the freedom fighters by the hospital nurse. From her also he hears about the city being freed from the imperialist's oppression. In this nationalist story the author has described Gandhi's historic fast and its influence on the national freedom struggle and on the international scene ravaged by II World War.

D.F. Karaka's *We Never Die* is a novel set against an Indian village and town depicts a stray picture of the Indian freedom movement through an innocent villager. The simple story of silent revolution of the Indian people in the slothful village life tries to solve the communalism inherent in the then society.

C.N. Zutsi's *Motherland: An Expository Novel of Modern India* is a novel depicting the threadbare and hackneyed story centring round the character of Mahatma Vikrama, who is a great national leader meant to symbolise Mahatma Gandhi, and his colleague Trilok. While Vikrama has an interview with Lord Addington, the then Viceroy of India for discussion on Indian problems, Trilok goes to help the Indians in South Africa where he is highly appreciated for his speeches that awaken the minds of these Indians. Trilok's wife Kamala also starts working on Congress principles. Mahatma Vikrama, having an interview with a representative of the "Gandhian" continues his struggle for Indian Independence.

The novelist says in his preface, "This expository novel is an attempt to portray a picture of certain aspects of actual life in modern India, and has been written with the definite purpose of awakening my own countrymen to this political plight under the foreign yoke." And by judicious mingling-mangling of romance and politics in the field of fiction, the novelist has portrayed something new in political literature and serves his purpose.

Conflict by Amir Ali is a novel centring round the 1942 "Quit India Movement." Through the character of Shankar, the novel portrays the involvement of student community and that of the villages in the Indian freedom struggle. This novel invites obvious comparison with *Kanthapura.* The story begins with the coming of Shankar, a 17 years old boy of Koregaon village, to a college in Bombay where he gradually develops political awareness and becomes a nationalist under Gandhi's influence. Shankar comes under the student leader Mehta's influence during the Independence movement. The police intervenes and Mehta and many other students are arrested and tortured. As a reaction to the All India Congress Committee session held in Bombay on 7 and 8 August 1942 all the prominent political leaders like Gandhi, Nehru, etc. are arrested and imprisoned. Consequently meetings, processions, hartals and strikes in the form of protest are arising out and all the student leaders are soon arrested while Shankar is left alone.

Shankar goes back to his village and organises the freedom movement there. The village mamlatdar is forced to leave the village and all the Government papers were burnt down by the crowd. Consequently, the Government police force inflicts tortures to the villagers. Another party of cruel soldiers appears and take away the men and rapes almost every woman in the village. Shankar escapes and sees his sweet heart Shanti's dead body. Seeing this Shankar remarks, "I will not repine, I will rebuild."[17] The story of Shankar founded on the historical struggle of 1942 has also another important aspect—the participation of the Muslims in the national struggle under the Congress.

R.N. Tagore's *Four Chapters* is a novel belonging to the last phase of his career. It is a remarkable novel bearing contemporaneous quality and here the novelist delivers an indictment on political fanaticism. The novelist describes it as a love story though it has a political background. It is comparable to *Romeo and Juliet*, a love-story founded on family feud and to *Doctor Zhivago*, a love-story set against the background of Soviet Revolution and Stalinist Reconstruction. The novel has the Terrorist Movement in Bengal in the first decade of this century as its background. The novel develops the nature and course of love between Atin and Ela—the hero and the heroine against the stormy background of revolutionary struggle and so it can be treated as a political novel.

Venu Chitale's *In Transit* covers an era of intense political activity in India and rise of Indian nationalism. The main character in the novel is Abba, a Patriarch of a type that is fast disappearing from our social life. So the narrative is spread over three generations. The novel depicts India's social and economic condition in transit and ends with the brave participation of Abba family's younger generation in the Civil Disobedience Movement and for which they have been jailed. It also describes the 1921 non-cooperation movement and the social life of Poona and Bombay with marriage, festival and death. Along with the venerable figure of the grand patriarch Abba, all the other characters—Dada, Lopamudra, Chander, Tai, Vahini, Bal,

Baban, Madhav, Mohana, Kusum, Nalini—are living, feeling, fighting and suffering in their own way for their country. The novel is treated as a political novel for its treatment of a heart-rending political struggle.

Zeenuth Futehally's *Zohra* is also a novel set against the political background of Hyderabad. It shows the changing panorama of Muslim social life in Hyderabad along with the freedom movement. The novel's mood is of a strong attachment to the national movement of the country and of reverence for Indian leaders fighting for her freedom.

There is a vivid reflection of modern politics and Gandhian movement in the story of a sensitive girl, Nawab Saheb's daughter Zohra's (which means the brightest star in all the Heavens) life whose face even in death was a face filtered through sorrow and suffering.

Anand's *Private Life of an Indian Prince* is a novel where the novelist aims to fuse contemporary political history with the personal history of a few individuals by hinting at the merger of the princely states with the Indian Union. The novel reflects an Indian state with its extravagant, debauched and voluptuous Prince Victor Edward George Ashok Kumar, one of the 600 Maharajas and Nawabs that Sardar Patel found on his hands in August 1947. This novel is a pathological study of this neurotic Maharaja of Shampur state who becomes neurotic under the terrible pulls and tensions of the two women of his harem and the unnerving political condition inside and outside his state during the post-Independence period when Patel was the home minister in charge of the States Department.

The prince squandered public money and passionately involved with concubine Ganga Dasi and also indulged in a series of affairs with other women by neglecting his good wife and children. He gradually lost control of his mind. The harassed subjects forming a Praja Mandal, a nationalist political organisation, compelled him to sign the instrument of Accession under the whim of Patel. Then the prince went to England where also he could not find peace. Soon he was summoned back to India for his implication in murdering Foolchand. At last he became totally insane and ended up in a lunatic asylum.

In this novel the machinations of the foreign power with whose help these princes dreamt of maintaining their sovereign independence, outside India and Pakistan, are also hinted at. The novelist has also looked at the national problem from the people's point of view which was identical to the Government's stand. What happened to prince Victor happened to almost all the Indian princes. And the corrupt atmosphere of Shampur palace is a faithful reproduction of what was going on in all other palaces of Indian states.

Narayan's *Waiting for the Mahatma* is a novel depicting a phase of Indian freedom struggle with Mahatma Gandhi in the last few years of his life among his followers. Here Gandhi is introduced as a character and not as a symbol amidst the events from 1941 to 1948 and action ranging from Malgudi to Delhi with Bharati-Sriram love story in the background. Since the stress is on Gandhi himself, we see him at Nallappa's grove in Malgudi and years later in Delhi in the fatal day of 30 January 1948. It is Bharati who makes Sriram a patriot and a man.

Here in this novel Gandhiji himself addresses political meetings in Malgudi. Indian people's activities following Gandhi's declaration of *Quit India Movement*; Gandhi's journey to Noakhali in the wake of partition and consequent suffering due to communal riots; his ashram life and his assassination are depicted here. Beginning with the period shortly before Indian Independence, showing a vast vista of political happenings of those days the novel closes with Gandhi's assassination. Narrating the love-story of two followers of Gandhi the novelist writes about the whole town of Malgudi in its impatient, and reverential waiting for the Mahatma when the Mahatma is on his South Indian tour. In fact, it is through and through a political novel projecting Gandhi as a character.

Abbas's *Inquilab* is a novel reflecting our freedom struggle commencing from the Rowlatt Bill and the Jallianwalla Bagh Massacre to the Salt Satyagraha and the Gandhi-Irwin Pact of 1931. All the important political events of the time are presented through the point of view of the hero Anwar who finds himself involved in them, though he is not committed to any of the political ideologies of the time—the ideology of the Congress or of the Muslim League. In the course of the story the Gandhian Revolutionary Age is projected with the works and sacrifices of Gandhi and other prominent Indian leaders. The hero Anwar is shifted from place to place, things happen to him and he is involved—like a leaf in the storm—in the political cataclysms of his time. There are discussions on the politics of the time by Anwar's father and his friends.

The Jallianwalla Bagh massacre arouses nationalist spirit in Anwar. His meeting with Gandhi and Nehru are turning points in his life. Nehru's speech in the Lahore Congress electrifies him. But his father has moved to the Muslim League while he believes in the nationalistic unity of the Hindus, the Muslims and the Christians and other communities for making India free from foreign yoke. The Hindu Muslim riots set his mind on fire.

Anwar helps his friend Ratan to get a pass which Ratan gives to Bhagat Singh to enter the Secretariat at Delhi and throw the bomb. The novel also describes Bhagat's trial and Subhas Bose's advent on the scene with the battle cry. The historic "Dandi March" and the brutal police atrocities are viewed with mixed emotion. He cannot stand up to all these things since his father and his uncle are fanning communal hatred. There are the Hindu and the Christian communists also. This communal frenzy makes havoc in Anwar's life and the nation's life. At last Anwar learns from his uncle that by fighting to save the Hindus he has shown his real blood. His uncle also disclosed that he is the son of Kaka Rameswar by a Muslim prostitute. It is the supreme movement of realisation for Anwar. N. Radhakrishnan rightly remarks:

"No doubt, *Inquilab* is a disturbing document of the soul stirring incidents of the period it describes."[18]

The novelist discusses certain vital issues involved in the freedom struggle. He mentions how the gap between the Hindus and the Muslims has been made. Depicting the entire fight for freedom, a Kaleidoscopic panorama of fast moving events each one episodic in nature and yet properly adjusted and composed in the general pattern of the freedom movement as its plot the novel has gained its rank among the Indian political novels.

Some Inner Fury by Kamala Markandaya is another novel dealing with the violent aspect of the professed non-violent-movement of 1942. The story begins with the return of Mira's brother Kit with his Oxford friend Richard. Kit becomes an I.C.S. officer while Richard becomes an A.D.C. Premala is Kit's dutiful wife and Mirabai falls in love with Richard. Govind is an adopted brother of Mira and Roshan is a rich lady who angles in the troubled waters of emancipation and revolutionary politics. Hickey, the Englishman is a missionary. Govind, wishing to escape from his hopeless love for Premala, becomes a revolutionary. All these characters are caught in the cells of the struggle.

The earlier part of the novel deals with the family of Kit and others. But soon tragedy descends upon the family when Govind and his companion burn a school run by Hickey who is helped by Premala in his humanitarian work. In that fire Premala gets suffocated and dies. Kit comes to the rescue of his wife but he also dies of a knife wound on the spot. Govind is charged for this murder and while a case is being tried for this by a jury a violent and furious mob rushes in and kills Hickey and Richard. Now Mira is left alone to be shut up with the ghosts of her memories. The novel is engineered by politics and in it the main characters transcend the bludgeonings of political mischance and assert the unconquerable spirit of humanity. In this novel, excluding Kit and Richard, all the characters are involved directly in political action.

Anand Lall in his *The House at Adampur* captures some of the events of the Nationalist Movement. He takes us to Delhi to show how the Nationalist Movement affected an upper-class family. The title is derived from a pleasure house at Adampur where Raja Muzaffer Khan maintains his harem. Set against the background of the political struggle of non-violence beginning from 1930 and ending in 1944, the story covers many epochs of the great struggle like the no-salt tax campaign which has rocked the whole of Delhi.

The political drama begins with the organisation of meetings in relation to Mahatma's "Dandi March" by Jai Singh, a lawyer and Shanti Devi. Huge crowds gather near Jamuna to manufacture salt. A severe lathi-charge follows and Shanti's daughter Lena and Jai Singh are hurt. Lena becomes Jai's nurse while Jai falls unconscious. She falls in love with him. Jai leaves for his village on receipt of a telegram of his mother's death. In his village Jai devotes to the rural upliftment programmes. Thus the novel reflecting the Gandhian Salt Satyagraha and Quit India Movement, grasps the nationalist theme and claims a strong Indian political novel.

A Time to be Happy by Nayantara Sahgal is also a novel dealing with two North Indian families during the last stages of the freedom struggle and the arrival of independence. The main theme here is the awakening of young Sanad, the "Brown Englishman" to the social and political realities of newly Independent India. In this novel we see the changes in the lives of the landlord class with their love for the values of the Mughal feudal world and the anglicised Indians evolved during the British rule caring for Western way of life and material propriety along with the winning of the country's freedom. These changes are observed through the eyes of a hardcore nationalist freedom fighter and earnest disciple of Gandhi and he himself is the narrator of the story; and so the story takes a profound political colour. There are many references to Congress activities and the events of 1942 in this novel. It depicts the lives of the educated upper-class people living in the period covering the non-cooperation movement, August disturbances in 1942, the Bengal famine and the great year 1947, the year of freedom. The national movement touching the novel at different points makes it a political novel.

Khushwant Singh's *I Shall Not Hear The Nightingale* is a novel set against the freedom movement and the war years from April 1942 to April 1943, the disturbed pre-partition period at Jallianwalla Bagh in the Punjab. The novel vividly presents an ironic picture of a Sikh joint-family illustrative of different Indian reactions to the freedom movement of the forties. It deals with the period of the "Quit India" conflagration. Sardar Buta Singh, the head of a Sikh family, a senior Magistrate is on the side of the British Government. His son Sher becomes a terrorist belonging to a terrorist group of students. Buta's illiterate wife looks after the welfare of the family. Sher's terrorist activities lead him to the murder of a police informer because a Sikh peasant starts blackmailing Sher and his companions. Sher is arrested but released later on in view of his father's faithful service and of the high regard of Mrs. Taylor, the Deputy Commissioner's wife, for the wife of Buta Singh, Sher's mother. Thus the relations between bureaucracy and the people naturally seem more than strained.

S. Menon Marath's *Wound of Spring* is also a novel showing the impact of change on a matriarchal Nayar family in Malabar during the nineteen twenties at the time of Moplah rising. The novelist shows his national consciousness in his choice of this particular period as the setting of this novel. The disintegration of the social system is depicted through the family episode at Trichur when the political movement is at its peak in that region. In this novel Parvati Amma, her son Govindan, and Unni and the whole clan are vividly portrayed. The novel has an ironical picture of the Gandhian movement. There is shown the bonfire of foreign made clothes at which beggars clamour: "Don't burn them, give them to us; and students welcome the agitation because the undone homework would not humiliate today, at any rate." The 1921 Moplah rebellion shapes the event in the narrative.

K. Nagarajan's *Chronicles of Kedaram* is another novel in which Gandhi appears as a character. The novel is set against the hectic period of freedom struggle in pre-Independence India. On this political backdrop a family chronicle in Kedaram, a South Indian town, is developed in the story. The novel depicts the pattern of life, both personal and political of a few persons of various callings in India of the period from 1925 to 1939.

This story of a South Indian district town, its Congress and its elections, is narrated by Gokarna Sastri (Koni), a lawyer, an orthodox Brahmin. He is friend and colleague of Vasudev Suri (Vasu) who is modern, well-dressed and broad minded. The highlights of the story are the feuds between the two Iyengar factions solved by Gandhi; and the so-called Nirmala Chari-Vasu affairs and the two election campaigns. This naive novel does not directly deal with the nationalist movement. We see Gandhi too as Koni sees him. But Gandhi appears with his ceaseless effort for the personal welfare of each individual and of the nation in general.

Attia Hosain's *Sunlight on a Broken Column* is a novel depicting the growth of the heroine Laila's personal life against the background of those confused times of the two decades before and after Independence. Covering a period of twenty years of the life of Laila, the narrator heroine, the novel is divided into four parts—the first part showing Laila as a girl of fifteen in a rich orthodox Muslim family, the second part showing her of the age of 19, the third part full of political activities, agitations, discussions, elections, etc., part IV taking up the story 14 years later. The period of 14 years reflects a critical period of Indian history with the outbreak of II World War, formation of Indian National Army, 1942 Agitation, Communal riots, Indian Independence and partition. Thus, showing the changing twenty years' life of Laila this novel also shows India's change from colonialism to Independence.

Manohar Malgonkar's *Combat of Shadows* is a novel depicting not only the social prejudice and hatred between the Britishers and the Indians but also Indian politicians selling out the national cause for their profit and self-interest without any moral scruples. Over and above these, many political situations in India of the time when the momentum of freedom struggle is obtained, are shown here.

Malgonkar's *The Princes* is an illustration of political fiction in which the action and the characters are so firmly grounded in politics. The novel gives a picture of the troubled times of the merger of the princely states into the Indian Union, with special reference to the small North Indian imaginary state of Begwad. The story is narrated by Abhayraj, the crown prince of Begwad. He is an insider-outsider viewing the entire merger drama as both actor and spectator. Abhay, a youth firmly rooted in age-old tradition and yet aware of the fast changing political scene, is shown as a foil to his feudal minded father the Maharaja. The feudal representative Maharaja Hiroji is a manly man capable of confronting, unarmed, a hostile mob and he thinks death to be better than humiliation at the hands of the forces that crush him. The author portrays him to have all the vices typical of his class. There is an intermingling of romance and adventure, heroism and chivalry; and through all these the novel depicts the trampling down of the ancient and viable Indian administrative set up for the new spirit of democracy.

Anand's *Death of a Hero*: *Epitaph for Maqbool Sherwani* depicts the crucification of Maqbool Sherwani, a Kashmiri freedom fighter, during the first invasion of Kashmir by Pakistani raiders in 1947. This novel does not reflect the faithful political developments since it is concerned with only the effect of the crisis on people's mind of that area.

Maqbool, the hero of the novel flees to Srinagar when the Pakistani raiders invade Kashmir. He is ordered to go back to Baramula to organise resistance. But he is too late and captured, tried and killed. The novel has a potential theme that can come upto the classic magnitude. But the author fails to bring up this theme upto the marked level. In this story Maqbool's mission is vague except his success on haranguing friends and getting captured afterwards. In spite of the novel's failure in etching the political developments in detail and systematically, this novel has succeeded in delineating the idea of Indian stance by representing through debates and conversations the attitude of the pro-Pakistani leaders and the viewpoints of Maqbool Sherwani, the protagonist of the (Indian) Kashmir National Conference.

R.K. Narayan's *Vendor of Sweets* is the representative novel in which Gandhi's followers appear visibly. In this novel Jagan is shown as a true disciple of Gandhi with a hypocritical oddity. He is proud of being called a Gandhian. He has high regard for Gandhi as his master. Though he earns a thousand rupees a day he leads a simple life. He has lost his wife and has only his son to take care of. In Jagan we see a person who cashes in on the image of Gandhi and his freedom struggle. Jagan can recollect all that Gandhi has said about various issues. To show that he is an ardent follower of Gandhi he speaks of putting on Khadi, of spinning of the Charkha, of the reading of the Gita and of the repeating of some of the statements of Gandhi.

Bhabani Bhattacharya's *Shadow from Ladakh* is a novel in which Gandhian ideal is represented by Satyajit Sen. Really, Satyajit, trained in Gandhi's Sevagram, is presented a victor in his resistance of steel town annexing Gandhigram. The triumph is brought by Satyajit through Gandhian non-violence, Satyagraha and fast unto death.

Chaman Nahal's fifth novel *The Crown and the Loincloth* deals with the theme of confrontation between the mighty British Empire (The Crown) and a resurgent India under the dynamic leadership of Mahatma Gandhi (The Loincloth) during 1915-22. The aspirations and ideas, dreams and enchantments, and frustrations and affirmations of middle class intelligentsia during those historically convulsive years are fictionalised in the novel. Set against the historical background and with some important historical figures, this novel depicts the quest for meaning and the endless possibilities inherent in human life by an individual.

The novelist makes Gandhi-Sunil equation by drawing Sunil as a model Gandhi in this story of the transmutation of the ordinary into the heroic and extraordinary. Sunil's wife Kusum is also depicted as parallel to Kasturba Gandhi. Gandhi's return to India in 1915 after his turbulent career in South Africa is shown here in the very first chapter of the novel along with his major encounters and experiences. As a political novel its importance lies in its typicality, that is, of fictionalising a political biography with a moralistic message.

3. Political Novels based on Partition Riots

The attainment of Indian freedom was followed by the tragic drama of Partition. India was left bleeding for sometime. It was perhaps the darkest period in the history of modern India which witnessed a movement of hatred and bigotry of men who had been living like brothers for centuries. In those days trains were arriving in Lahore Station packed with butchered passengers with messages scribbled on the sides of the carriage: "A present from India." This made the Muslims react heroically in sending back trainloads of butchered Sikhs and Hindus with the legend: "A present from Pakistan." Naturally these ghastly developments find expression in Indo-Anglian fiction. This tragic drama of partition inspired many remarkable novels like Khushwant Singh's *Train To Pakistan,* Raj Gill's *The Rape,* Manohar Malgonkar's *A Bend in the Ganges,* Chaman Nahal's *Azadi,* etc. These novels are based on the insane butcheries committed in the name of religion before and after partition.

Train To Pakistan is a novel reflecting the picture of the bestial horrors enacted on the Indo-Pakistan border region during the terror haunted days of partition. It is the story of Mano Majra, a village on the Indo-Pak border. The routine of a peaceful, if uneventful, existence of the villagers—Sikhs and Muslims—is sketched at the beginning of the story. The hero Juggut (popularly known as Jugga) is a busy Sikh youth regarded as a bad fellow in that village.

The actual story begins with house-breaking and robbery and the murder of the village moneylender, Lala Ramlal, the only Hindu of the village by a gang of dacoits. Jugga is suspected of that murder. But at that time Jugga is away from home as he is with his sweet-heart Nooran, the daughter of the old Imam of the village mosque. Upto this time Muslims and Sikhs are leading a life of happy communal harmony. The murder of Lala Ramlal offered a shrewd magistrate, Hukum Chand (D.C. of Mano Majra, getting drunk and pawing the hired Muslim prostitute, Haseena) the chance to manipulate it as he likes. A trainload of dead bodies of Sikhs and Hindus comes from Pakistan and this inflames the communal frenzy of the Sikhs. Then the Sikhs hold a meeting. Local Muslims are evacuated to a nearby refugee camp at that time. The Sikh leader boy tells the villagers that a trainload of Muslims is to cross the bridge on the river Sutlej the next day, and they should kill all those Muslims. Even the reminder that the Muslim brethren of Mano Majra village will go to Pakistan by that train cannot stop them now from the execution of the plot.

The Sikhs planned to stretch a rope across the bridge just one foot above the funnel of the engine. This means that all the four hundred or five hundred Muslims on the roof of the train will be swept into the river by the rope. Accordingly the next night the Sikhs await the coming of the train in tense anticipation. But Jugga reaches the spot. As the train arrives he climbs on the bridge and stretches on the rope while other Sikhs awaiting the disaster see this and fire shots at him. Before he falls down dead under the oncoming train he has cut the rope with his "kirpan" (sword). Thus, this "Number 10 Badmash" Juggut saves many Muslim lives at the cost of his own life. This sacrifice of Juggut Singh to save Nooran and the awakening of compassion in the magistrate Hukum Chand's heart for a young Muslim prostitute represent the still sad voice of humanity amid the pointless brutality and frenzy.

This politically dramatic novel conveys a hint of the grossness, ghastliness and total insanity of the two-nation theory and partition tragedy with its pity and terror. The disruption of the communal harmony and fellow-feeling inherent in Indian society by the vested interests for the communities' own ends at that critical juncture of winning freedom is vividly depicted in this novel.

B. Rajan's *The Dark Dancer* is a novel reflecting the last phase of the freedom struggle and partition holocaust.

Manohar Malgonkar's fourth novel *A Bend in the Ganges* is a political novel reflecting the bloody political event of the partition against which is set the personal story of Debi Dayal, Gian and Sundari. The depiction of the Gandhian non-violent movement and the terrorist movement forms the political aspect in this novel.

The novel depicts the great human drama of uprooting countless homes and driving of millions of people from one country to another in the aftermath of partition. The novelist works on a large canvas with scenes changing from India to the Andamans and back and his racy narrative is full of excitement. Panoramic in scope and epic in aspiration, this novel is crowded with events of modern Indian political history beginning with the Civil Disobedience Movement of the thirties and ending in the post-partition riots in the Punjab. The narrative is packed with such excitements as the boycott of foreign goods, the secret activities of terrorist groups, the outbreak of the second World War, the Japanese occupation of the Andamans, the British retreat from Rangoon, the long march evacues from Burma, the Bombay dock explosion, the dismemberment of India, etc.

In fact, in this action packed novel the action ranges from domestic bloodshed to national tragedy, both being represented by the tussle and the bloodshed between the Big House and the Little House of Himachal Pradesh village Konshet that open the novel and the epic scale bloodshed killing millions of men, women, children, the Hindus and the Muslims in the time of Partition that ensues this novel. All characters are concerned with national movement for independence and the novelist gives balanced views on the discussions about the nonviolence, patriotism and communalism. Thus dealing with the theme of two different ideologies—violence and non-violence against the historical and political background of partition this novel can be treated as a political novel.

Another important partition novel is Chaman Nahal's *Azadi*. It deals with the theme of the partition of India that held the subcontinent in a nightmare of horror, communal bloodshed, mass massacres, rapes, abductions, and the vast influx of refugees. Spanning the period from the announcement of the Cabinet Mission Plan on June 3, 1947 to the 'aftermath,' the murder of Mahatma Gandhi on January 30, 1948, the novel dramatises the impact of the momentous events of political history on a few individuals. The novel gives an account of the migration of Lala Kanshi Ram, a Sialkot grain merchant and his family to India which has neither accommodation nor work for the vast hordes pouring in everyday. In fact, this novel gives one of the most comprehensive fictional accounts of the partition holocaust in Indian English literature.

The first part shows the peaceful life of Lala Kanshi Ram's family in Sialkot which is turning into the grim struggle of migration. The second part shows the communal riots in Sialkot making the Hindus suffer robbery, rape and massacre. There is a realistic and effective presentation of scenes in this part like the horrible condition in the refugee camp in Pakistan, the queer parade of naked Hindu women in Narowal, the immolation of Niranjan Singh and the attacks of the Muslim fanatical mobs on Hindu refugees, Arun's witnessing the hair-raising scene of the rape of beautiful Sunanda and his killing the rapist captain Rahmat Ullah Khan, etc. Besides, this novel portrays the tragic exodus vividly. Thus, the novel possesses the qualities of being a partition novel.

Raj Gill's *The Rape* is a novel set against the background of partition and depicting two lovers of a Sikh village called Lyallpur. The story is interwoven with the effects of partition on an otherwise placid village—their reactions to the national movement, the subsequent measures they take to meet the "Muslim Menace," their exodus and settling down in an Indian village and the love-affair between the hero and two of the girls with whom he falls in love. There are two heroines, one to commit suicide and another to be raped by the hero's father. Thus this novel reflects the horrid aspects of human life, following the partition holocaust.

4. Political Novels based on post-Independence Political Themes/Issues

There has been an endless stream of political novels in Indian literature. Even in the Post-Independence Indian literature the tradition of writing political novels is prevalent. Various events of national importance like the liberation of Goa, the Indo-Pakistan war of 1965, the Indo-Chinese War of 1962, the Indo-Bangladesh war of 1971, etc. have occurred in the political firmament of the post-Independence India. These events have been the source and inspiration of many of the political novels of the post-Independence Indian literature.

One of the remarkable political novels based on the post-Independence political firmament is Lambert Mascarenhas's *Sorrowing Lies My Land.* It is a novel depicting the freedom struggle in Goa in the years preceding Goa's liberation in 1961. Upto 1961 Goa was a Portuguese colony although the Goans were Hindus. The story of the novel shows a Goan gentleman farmer Tobias's involving in the Goan struggle for freedom. He becomes the leading figure when the revolution gathers momentum. Soon the Portuguese administrators bring the reign of terror into the land while Tobias and his party suffer terribly but they remain undaunted. The Portuguese inflict torture to the people and rape Goan girls. At last Tobias is arrested and his own son Robert gives evidence against him when he is tried.

This act of a son's giving evidence against his father as well as the act of raping Milena, a Goan girl by the Portuguese soldiers are terrible and poignant incidences. In the end one of Tobias's sons enters the church, another goes to Africa, his wife dies and thus he is deprived of his supports one by one. At last he dies under a pitiable condition but heroically and with the hope that his land that lies sorrowing will one day be free and happy.

Nayantara Sahgal's *This Time of Morning, Storm in Chandigarh, The Day in Shadow* and *A Situation in New Delhi* are all political novels set against the political scenes and depicting some well-known figures in the Indian political arena of the post-Independence era.

This Time of Morning deals with politics in the last days of Nehru's Prime Ministership. The story narrates the fall of Kalyan Singh, an important figure in Government. Much of the action takes place in Delhi and its corridors of power like the houses of ministers, politicians and others. In this novel we see a happy fusion of political and domestic themes. In the political aspect the author depicts how the pre-Independence politicians have degenerated into power mongering, career-hunting and intriguing opportunist after Independence when personal clashes between the so-called leaders are passed off as ideological differences, thus turning personal issues into national ones. The post-Independence selfishness and dirty politics are reflected in this novel and in it the novelist attempts at presenting India of mature democracy.

The setting of *Storm in Chandigarh* is Chandigarh, the common capital of the Punjab and Haryana. The political background is that of the division of the Punjab into the Sikh dominated Punjab and the largely Hindu state of Haryana and that of common capital Chandigarh is becoming an apple of discord between the two states and the two chief ministers—Harpal Singh of Haryana and Gyan Singh of the Punjab regarding the occupation of Chandigarh.

The Day in Shadow deals with the theme of new leadership

ousting the old. Sumer Singh, Deputy Minister for Petroleum, and the stern, unbending Senior Minister for petroleum are well-carved out political figures. In fact, this novel reflects the present-day Delhi, the pace of change, the passing of Gandhism, the defiant amoralism of the jet-set, the new style of politics, the chronic sense of uncertainty, etc.

A Situation in New Delhi also deals with the aftermath of Nehru's death, the Naxalite Movement and student unrest. In this novel Shivraj (identified as Jawaharlal Nehru) and his sister Devi are vividly portrayed figures dominating the scene of action. Indeed Sahgal can give a touch of authenticity and maturity of her art to this novel.

Midnight's Children by the Indian born Salman Rushdie (published in the U.K. and the U.S.A.) is a political novel dealing with the political history of India from the time of the Jallianwalla Bagh to the end of the Emergency in 1977. The title refers to the children born in the midnight hour of India's "Tryst with Destiny" on 15 August 1947.

The story is narrated by one Saleem Sinai, the hero of the novel and one of the 580 children born in the time and suffered with an exceptional fate in their nativity. Spreading over six decades and spatially over all India, Pakistan and Bangla Desh the novel shows Saleem's ordinary—extraordinary life and projects the multitudinous opulence and variegatedness of life in India, the squalor, confusion, exasperation, and equally the vitality, charity and silent heroism of the millions. The book has thirty chapters in its three part. In part I, the narrative goes back to the time of Jallianwalla Bagh tragedy and it ends with the birth of Saleem Sinai, the narrator hero, on the fateful midnight of 15 August 1947. Part II begins with the birth of the hero and concludes with the end of the Indo-Pakistan War on 23 September 1965. In part III, the narrative comes forward to the end of the Emergency in March 1977.

The above thematic study of the Indo-Anglian political novels shows that the form of these novels is alien while their content is Indian. Presentation of revolutionary motif of the Indians, Indian people's involvement in the freedom movement, national uprising against the foreign rule, the pivotal role of Mahatma Gandhi in the freedom struggle with his non-violence and Satyagraha, delineation of characters representing political and socio-political ideals, discussion on the socio-political issues and problems, etc., are some of the common characteristics of these novels. Moreover, their plots are too mechanical and their style is also too much Indianised by using a lot of vocabulary from the author's mother-tongue.

This summary of the novels is intended to serve as a background and point of reference for the study of Bhabani Bhattacharya's novels. It is not intended as an evaluative criterion but as a context. Bhattacharya's novels, so unlike the novels the Western reader is accustomed to, make sense only in this context.

REFERENCES

1. Morris E. Speare, *The Political Novel, Its Development in England and America* (New York: Oxford University Press, 1966), ix.
2. H.A.L. Fisher, "The Political Novel," Quoted by Gordon Milne, *The American Political Novel* (Norman: University of Oklahoma Press, 1966), 4.
3. Joseph L. Blotner, *The Political Novel* (New York: Doubleday, 1955), 2.
4. Irving Howe, *Politics and the Novel* (New York: Horizon Press, 1957), 19.
5. M.K. Naik, *Dimensions of Indian English Literature* (New Delhi: Sterling Publishers, Pvt. Ltd., 1984), 116.
6. Mahadev L. Apte, "The Political Novel in Marathi," *Politics and the Novel in India* edited by Yogendra K. Malik (New Delhi: Orient Longman, 1978), 75-76.
7. Velcheru Narayan Rao, "The Political Novel in Telegu," *Politics and the Novel in India,* edited, Yogendra K. Malik (New Delhi: Orient Longman, 1978), 94.
8. Bhupal Singh, *A Brief Survey of Anglo-Indian Fiction* (London: Oxford University Press, 1934), 306.
9. Krishna Rao, A.V., *The Indo-Anglian Novel and the Changing Tradition* (Mysore: Rao & Raghavan, 1972), 21.

10. Radhakrishnan, N., *Indo-Anglian Fiction: Major Trends and Themes* (Madras: Emerald Publishers, 1984), 13.
11. Krishna Kripalani, *Modern Indian Literature* (Bombay: Nirmal Sadanand Publishers, 1968), 79-80.
12. Minakshi Mukherjee, *The Twice Born Fiction* (New Delhi: Arnold-Heinemann, 1971), 61.
13. P.P. Mehta, *Indo-Anglian Fiction: An Assessment* (Bareilly: Prakash Book Depot, 1979), 138.
14. G.P. Sharma, *Nationalism in Indo-Anglian Fiction* (New Delhi: Sterling Publishers, 1978), 201.
15. G.P. Sarma, *Nationalism in Indo-Anglian Fiction* (New Delhi: Sterling Publishers, 1978), 205.
16. M.K. Naik, *Dimensions of Indian English Literature* (New Delhi: Sterling Publishers, 1984), 119.
17. Amir Ali, *Conflict* (Bombay: National Information and Publication Ltd., 1947), 167.
18. N. Radhakrishnan, *Indo-Anglian Fiction: Major Trends and Themes* (Madras: Emerald Publishers, 1984), 38.

3

The Novels: Critical Appraisal

1. *So Many Hungers!*

Bhabani Bhattacharya's first novel *So Many Hungers!* was published in October 1947, two months after India's attainment of Independence. Since the novel saw the light of day at such a momentous period in the history of the country, one would naturally expect freedom to be the theme of the novel. And indeed it is. Regarding the theme of the novel G.P. Sarma remarks:

> Bhabani Bhattacharya's *So Many Hungers!* is not only the last political novel about the freedom struggle of this period (the early forties) but also one of the best of this category.[1]

In this novel he refers to the people's hunger for food and for freedom. So this twin hunger is dealt with as the central theme of the novel. Inter-twisting the Bengal Famine of 1943 and the Quit India Movement of 1942 the novelist makes relevant references to these dual aspects, firstly, with Kishore's song which has a deep significance:

> I know, I know, beloved,
> Not in this life will hungers be sated
> I know, I know, beloved:[2]

And secondly, with the inspiring note of a Tagore song with which the novel concludes:

> The more they tighten the chains,
> The more the chains loosen![3]

Of the two intertwined themes of freedom and hunger, the theme of hunger figures more prominently and it outweighs the other in content.

But a close analysis of the novel will show that the title *So Many Hungers!* is amply justified, because the novel indeed shows many hungers: for food, for affection, for love, for lust, for money, for name and fame, for sacrifice, for political freedom, for imperial expansion, for human dignity and self-respect, for the general welfare of all and for spiritual weapon as employed by the hunger strikers and Devata fasting unto death.

Haunted by the biggest ever, man-made famine in Bengal in 1943 and the historic 'Quit India Movement' of the preceding year Bhattacharya depicts the naked horror of the famine-stricken peasants in the background of Gandhian Satyagraha struggle, the twin themes being shown in the two families to which Kajoli and Rahoul belonged respectively.

The novel has a composite plot weaving out of two main strands—the story of Samarendra Basu's family with young Rahoul as the principal character and the story of the peasant family with the young girl Kajoli as the central character. The two stories represent the freedom movement and the agonies of the famine respectively.

The two stories are joined by the common character Devesh Basu, who is the *de jure* head of the Basu family and the *de facto* head of the peasant family. Leaving his son and grand-sons rolling in the luxurious city life, he lives a very simple village life with the family of Kajoli at Baruni. Moreover, he is the source of inspiration to both Rahoul and Kajoli, the two central characters of the novel. About the two main strands in the plot of the novel K.R. Chandrasekharan rightly states:

> "Rahoul's story is a representation in miniature of the struggle for Freedom. The sad tale of Kajoli is likewise a pathetic record of what happened to more than two million men and women who became victims of a famine, which was not an act of God, but which was

> brought about by the rapacity and selfishness of profiteers and the indifference of an alien Government."[4]

First, it is the story of Dr. Rahoul, Samarendra Basu's first son, an astro-physicist in the university of Calcutta. Before his obtaining D.Sc. degree from Cambridge he had contemplated joining the Independence Movement and courting arrest under the influence of his grandfather Devesh Basu. This story unfolds his gradual development as a freedom fighter on Gandhian lines. About his role as a freedom fighter Chandrasekharan fittingly remarks:

> "He is a staunch nationalist and he cannot forget the hypocrisy of the foreign rulers who talk about the Four Freedoms which, so far as India is concerned, do not include the freedom to be free."[5]

In the opening of the book this Cambridge educated intellectual, busy in the study, research and teaching, is very upset by the war gradually spreading to Bengal. But he believes that the death of millions of young men will surely bring about a new world order. Thus Rahoul's faith in the lofty and finer values of life depicts his optimistic views of life.

Chapter 2 opens with a bright new day, filling Rahoul with the high hope that sacrifice purifies human beings. So in spite of his being the son of a profiteer he offers free help to the famished people and pregnant women when the man-made famine stalks Bengal. Kunal, Rahoul's younger brother, a spirited, adventurous youngman, affectionate and cheerful and embodying noble ideals and values appears only in the earlier part of the novel. Nothing is heard about him after his leaving home for service in North Africa and Italy as a junior army officer.

Samarendra Basu, nominally a lawyer but a well-to-do fellow is quite opposite in nature and ways of life to his saintly father. He is greedy without even a tinge of patriotism in him. His only aim is to please his British rulers to earn titles and to accumulate a huge wealth. By forming a trading concern with the ironic name "Cheap Rice Limited" he collects rice and hoards it, and later on sells it at very high price. He is proud of his son's D.Sc. degree and he wants his son to hold the highest post of Technical Adviser in New Delhi. But at the end of the novel Samarendra's dream-castle is broken to pieces when the report of Kunal missing somewhere in Italy and the news of Rahoul's arrest for joining the Quit India Movement come simultaneously to him.

Samarendra's father Devesh Basu known as Devata is the proto-type of Gandhi in action in Baruni village. He is very much loved and venerated by the villagers. He has infused Rahoul with trust in existence. Devata represents ideal life with all its dignity, courage, grandeur and strength. Whoever contacts with him is infused with hope and strength. He always thinks about the welfare of the villagers. So he advises them not to sell their rice to government agents. Thus he tries to resist the exploitation of the war situation. Gandhi's political agitation gathers momentum in Baruni also because Devata urges the people not to pay taxes to the unjust rulers.

Secondly, it is the story of Kajoli, a girl from the peasant family of Baruni where Devata has settled down. The story focuses on Kajoli and members of her family who are reduced to destitution because of the man-made famine. Kajoli's father and his elder son Kanu have been arrested for their joining the Civil Disobedience Movement. But Devata takes Kajoli's mother as his daughter and Kajoli as his granddaughter. He now becomes the head of the family.

Devata encourages the villagers in the freedom struggle by advising them not to use violence. In the early part of the novel Devata is arrested and on the eve of his arrest he exhorts the villagers to be strong, true and deathless. Then he is taken to Dehra Dun jail where he undertakes a fast unto death when the Quit India Movement is at its zenith. The news of this fast flashed in newspapers reaches Kajoli on that fateful morning when she decides to become a prostitute. Suddenly recollecting his parting words and advice she drops her decision and saves herself from ignominy and shame. Thus, Devata is her guardian angel.

In Kajoli we see Bhattacharya's characteristic portrayal of a highly idealised Indian woman fully representing the image of the new woman heralded by Gandhian thought. She is the novelist's main focus and conveyer of his message, an incarnation of faith in the nobleness and fullness of life inheriting the fundamental values and manners of India, unaffected and undefiled by modern attitudes and notions.

The stories of Rahoul and Kajoli are intertwined to expose both the themes of freedom and hunger. Rahoul is left untouched by the government on the plea of the possibility of his discovering the Death Ray although the government knows his nationalistic leanings. Since his mind has been clearly impressed by his grandfather's Gandhian ideas he inclines to join the people to fight for freedom.

Soon after it the leaders are arrested and imprisoned one after another. The arrest and trial of Nehru in Gorakhpur has stirred the country and his statement during the trial inspired the people. Now Rahoul also metamorphoses from an academic city elite to a traditional devoted freedom fighter. After seeking advice from his grandfather in Dehra Dun Central jail he plunges into the Quit India Movement and proclaims the British cessation of India.

Early one morning a black police van drives upto the Relief Centre where Rahoul has been feeding the destitutes so far and takes him away to jail. At the prison gate he is joined by other prisoners and in their march into the prison they sing in unison Tagore's memorable words: "The more they tighten the chains, the more the chains loosen." Thus closes the novel with the close of Rahoul's story associating with all sections of men's voluntary seeking imprisonment for the country's freedom.

Besides this theme of political freedom the theme of hunger for food comes to the forefront and steals the limelight. It is the story of sufferings in the Kajoli family symbolising the cruel fate of rural Bengal population. Kajoli, sprightly and innocent girl of 14 lives with her unnamed mother and younger brother Onu. Devata adopts this family and shares their plain meal.

The tragedy of the innocent Kajoli family is the premonition and symbolic shape of devastation affecting the whole Bengal. The fishing boats are destroyed by the government. Many villagers are evacuated and peasants are forced to sell their grain to the government agents and greedy hoarder. Thus they are reduced to paupers whose life becomes a tale of woe and the end of one tale is the beginning of another.

Soon men, women and children sink down and die. The destitute humanity begins to pour into the rich city in tens of thousands—misery's overflow from the countryside. But the pity of the villagers' plight is that they will fight and die over a moral issue. The hunger is their fate, an expiation of the sins of past lives. After the arrest of Devata along with other Congress workers of the village, the village has become rudderless while they have been imprisoned for burning the dakghar (post office).

Being quite helpless Kajoli now marries a youngman named Kishore. But her happiness is short-lived as Kishore is killed very soon in an accident on the railway embankment on his way to Calcutta. But his tragedy is unknown to the Kajoli family. By this time Kajoli is five months pregnant. They begin to live on roots, figs and whatever they can get for meal. They sell whatever can be sold, including the cow-bell adorning Mangala's neck. Brothel agents from Calcutta try to attempt Kajoli but she angrily rejects the offer. The mother offers Mangala to a fisherwoman attempting to bury her starving child alive. Now finding no possibility to live in the village, Kajoli, her mother and little brother Onu also join the endless cavalcade of starving masses towards Calcutta (Kolkata).

The sufferings met by the mother and her two children on their way to Calcutta (Kolkata) represent the plight of the many destitutes pouring into the city in search of food. On the way

Kajoli is raped by a sexually starving soldier leaving her to bleed helplessly. A jackal attempts to eat up Kajoli but Onu somehow drives it away. But the repentant soldier sends the girl in a military van, ready for an army doctor who gives her first aid and later takes care of her and the family, to Calcutta. Kajoli is admitted in the hospital while her mother and Onu eke out their living by begging as pavement dwellers.

Besides these things, the family experiences a lot of sufferings on the way and on the city's pavement. They come across famished skeletons groaning in pain while jackals crouch and eat their bodies. Vultures circle over the dead bodies and make a prey of human flesh. At times hungry people eat what the animals refuse to take. In this struggle for crumbs of food or dirt animals often prove stronger than the suffering folk. On one occasion Onu is defeated in his fight with a dog for possession of a jam-tin dug out from the rubbish. Boys fight with boys for scrap of food. A few relief centres including the one run by Rahoul provide food to limited numbers of destitutes. But Kajoli's mother is happy and grateful that Kajoli is at least temporarily in a hospital.

After her discharge from the hospital Kajoli decides to become a prostitute to maintain her family. She has planned to go with the betel woman, a brothel agent early next morning. By an ironic co-incidence her mother also has planned to commit suicide the same morning by jumping into the river from a bridge.

Early the same morning she goes with the betel woman to the brothel. On the way she hears the newspaper vendors shouting about Devata's fast unto death in the prison house at Dehra Dun. Remembering Devata's parting words she decides to earn an honest living by turning a newspaper vendor. She at once rejects the offer of the betel woman and refunds her money. While the woman is astounded Kajoli slaps her on the face and calls her "Jackal-woman." Thus closes the story of Kajoli.

Indeed, the novel unfolds the mental agonies of the people during the war period because of the misrule and wrong policies of the unfavourable British Government. The novel deals with the destiny of a whole populace and not that of an individual. Such aspects of disintegration and social cataclysm is shown in Boris Pasternak's *Doctor Zhivago*.

The novel has a compact and organic plot. All the incidents are related to the theme and evolved from the interaction of the characters and situations. It is clever of the novelist to use the two plots—the upper middle class Basus and the peasant family of Kajoli moving side by side to realistically represent the two poles of Bengalee society.

In regard to characterisation, the novelist attains success here too. Through the three main characters belonging to the same family—Devata, Samarendra and Rahoul—he has very skilfully depicted all three social forces that were at work then. Devata, a sincere lover of his country appears as a man of flesh and blood. Samarendra Basu, a profiteer and black marketeer is only anxious about the welfare of his two sons. Rahoul, a West-educated intellectual dragged into politics by the aspiration for freedom of the country, is finely carved out by the novelist as an individual of flesh and blood, who at the end of the novel becomes a Gandhian agitator.

Similarly, Bhattacharya portrays Kajoli's character as an embodiment of Gandhian ideas and tries to individualise her. Indeed, she is distinctly human but not mere ideal or type. Thus the novelist while dealing with a national crisis and widespread calamity, also enriches the story by portraying individual characters. But as for Kajoli's nameless mother and father, they may be taken as symbols or types. Here we may quote Chandrasekharan's remark:

> "Every character is not developed to the same extent for the ostensible reason that proper balance should be maintained between the story of a mass upheaval and the story of a few individuals."[6]

Bhabani Bhattacharya is successful in portraying woman characters. He presents the picture of Indian woman full of vitality, high ideals and a ray of hope for mankind. In this novel women are victimised as mother (the peasant mother) and wife (Manju and Kajoli) during the horrendous days of the great Bengal Famine. He also presents a victimised woman as a redeemer in the case of Kajoli's taking a decision to fight the procuress and to sell newspaper to maintain her family.

Woman as a symbol of sacrifice is shown in the character of Kajoli's mother attempting suicide to remove the burden of hunger from her children. The image of the westernised society lady of the urban and sophisticated circle is seen in a lady who is nicknamed as Madame Bareback.

Another remarkable quality of the novel is the novelist's use of imagination purposively. There is ample room for imaginative development of situation and episode in the plot of the novel. Many characters are sketched to be developing in imaginary situations. Many imaginary scenes and episodes are delineated as real and actual happenings.

Bhattacharya has used a distinctive quality of style in this novel. Using short, impassioned sentences weighed with emotion and meaning, and each balanced against the other he attracts the reader's attention. Indeed, his style is a distinguished, lucid and eloquent one, though it lacks the brilliance of Indian rhythm and sensibility which abounds in Raja Rao's novels.

Since the novelist has caught the vein of rural speech and the informal behaviour of the people, their rustic world and their small and simple views about the great things that take place around them, he uses ungrammatical and unidiomatic English. Besides, he uses many illiterate sentences to form the speech of many of his characters. He has used many Bengali expressions in his English but without any special value for such use, arousing the suspicion that he did not learn English well enough. Indeed his faulty grammar and inert diction disappoint the reader greatly.

But he has coined new compound words and sentences to suit his own purpose of highlighting the rural speech. Equally curious is his failure to use the auxiliary *do* for interrogative sentences. The exclamation mark in the title of the book is awkward, to say the least. His overuse of a number of short and ungrammatical sentences together forms a way that does not sound natural in English and it violates the language. But the use of heavy alliteration indicates the novelist's idea of desirable literary style. All this indicate a lack of literary culture in him.

2. *Music for Mohini*

Bhabani Bhattacharya's second novel, *Music for Mohini,* was published in 1952. Set against the background of the post-Independence India, this novel moves on two levels—the personal and the social. An analysis of the novel will show many tensions—between the mind of the husband and the body of the wife, between East and West, village and town, tradition and modernity, astrology and rationalism, daughter-in-law and mother-in-law. All these tensions are resolved ultimately suggesting the harmony of the music.

Viewed on the personal level, *Music for Mohini* dwells on the intellectual and emotional development of the heroine, Mohini, from care-free and sheltered girlhood to the position of wife and the mistress of a prominent and influential house with great traditions and orthodoxy. The novel begins with the depiction of the unaffected and happy life of the 17 years old girl Mohini studying at school. As the story progresses, she is seen to indulge in romantic fancies. Soon a marriage proposal comes from a handsome, well-educated and affluent young man in the late twenties named Jayadev, the head of the aristocratic family called the Big House in Behula village. With the approval of Mohini's father the marriage is arranged even without Jayadev and Mohini seeing each other.

The marriage ceremony is over and Mohini is transported from her modernistic city home to the new orthodox village home where she is received with formal rites suggesting her involvement in new responsibilities of a new world. Her mother-in-law is an austere, dedicated and iron-willed woman. Women of the family cannot sit down for a meal along with the men and music is tolerated only for the purpose of worship. Besides, Mohini's main problem in the family is her mental adjustment to her husband, because she who stands for vitality and life finds in Jayadev—"a silent, solitary man with heavy lidded dreamy eyes in a young tranquil face."[7] A scholar obsessed by his dream "to reorientate the values and patterns of Hindu life"[8] and an intellectual with a tireless quest for knowledge, he wishes to see his wife as Gargi or Maitreyi. He expects her to share his programme of social reform such as campaign against superstition, caste system and exploitation of women, etc.

Mohini's dream of reciprocal love between her husband and herself is shattered when she comes under the control of her widowed mother-in-law who epitomises Hindu orthodoxy and superstitions, any breach of which is a sacrilege to her. Jayadev is blind to her mother's mentality, which makes Mohini's life unbearable in the Big House. But her married sister-in-law, Rooplekha encourages her to cope with the situation by citing the example of her own married life which involves the need for synthesis of opposites and by making a wise remark:

> "We connect culture with culture, Mohini, our old Eastern view of life with the new semi-Western outlook.... This is more urgent today than ever before. Our new India must rest on this foundation."[9]

As Mohini stands for life she does not accept defeat. She resolves to bring happiness to the Big House by modifying her stand and by making adjustments in her role of wife. She begins to educate the village women. Thus she shares a common interest with her husband and thus brings them closer to find a harmony. Jayadev also tackles the crisis of famine completely and now there emerges a silent harmony between Jayadev and Mohini.

Mohini makes her adjustments with her mother-in-law and the Big House too. Entrusting her with the safe custody of money and jewellery, she also obeys her mother-in-law to drop the singing of secular song and to wear only cotton saries and gold bangles instead of lovely and fashionable bangles. In her imagination Mohini is haunted by the spirits of Jayadev's ancestors in the Big House and she desires to escape into freedom and light.

But a crisis arises in the Big House with Jayadev's approaching the age of twenty-eight, which is predicted by an astrologer to be the year of Jayadev's death unless he becomes a father. So his mother is anxious. She advises Mohini to offer blood from her bosom to the virgin Goddess to beget a child. At this critical juncture Jayadev is bitten by a non-poisonous snake, which at first causes alarm and consternation in the mind of the mother who takes it as a warning for Jayadev's death. To fulfil her role as a lady of the orthodox Big House Mohini accepts this ordeal. But she is saved from this ceremonial offering of blood in the nick of time by the arrival of Jayadev who gets wind of the affair from Sudha, the girl who dreams of marrying Jayadev. Thus, Jayadev's modern attitude defeats his mother's orthodoxy.

But this defeat of the mother coincides ironically with her victory since Mohini, at last, is prepared to adjust herself with the Big House and within her own mind and is ready to sacrifice everything including her husband's marriage of Sudha as a second wife. Fortunately, it is known that Mohini is already with child. This removes her fear of being replaced by Sudha. And life once again becomes a music for her. She feels fulfilled. Actually, her life is a throb of music made up of diverse notes. Thus with a psychological growth and change of outlook Mohini has re-established harmony within herself which fulfils the novelist's purpose of bridging over the gulf between the old and the new.

The novel also deals with the basic hungers related to man-woman relationship. Every young woman and man has an innate urge for a lover. This urge is seen in the case of girls like Mohini, Reba, Bindu and bachelor Harindra all of whom desire to have a mate of her or his own choice. Through Mohini and Jayadev we see young wife and husband's yearning for the joyful company of each other. The hunger for an intellectual's quest for knowledge is seen in Jayadev. Mohini's hunger for food while going to her husband's and the passing reference to the Bengal Famine of 1943 are examples of man's hunger for food.

Bhattacharya also spot-lights other kinds of hunger such as the worshipper's hunger for God, the barren woman's longing for a child and the lonely wife's craving for her husband, etc. through a folk-song sung by a cart-man. Here Bhattacharya seems not merely repeating the theme of *So Many Hungers*! but trying to highlight other aspects of hunger lying deeper in the human nature.

Viewed on the social plane, the novel concentrates upon social freedom, which is all important for the real progress of the orthodox and superstitious people of India. Hence, the hero of the novel, Jayadev is shown to be dedicated to social reform and freedom. To quote Dr. B. Shyamala Rao:

> "The novel *Music for Mohini* is a true replica of the India of the Post-war Independence still making abortive attempts to come out of the mire of tradition and orthodoxy."[10]

In fact, the need for a change of social outlook and reorientation of social values in India is the novelist's major concern. Orthodoxy is depicted through the characters of old Mother and Jayadev's mother, Old Mother is against recording Mohini's song for commercial purpose. She prevents Mohini from going to an English Convent School and she also rejects a marriage proposal for the disrespect shown by the suitor's party. Again, bride showing and bride inspection, as if she is a commodity, before the family of the prospective groom, the practices of not touching food by a bride during marriage till the whole ceremony is over, waiting on her husband, not talking during meal, aversion to allopathic medicines and injections, untouchability and frowning upon widow remarriage are listed in the novel to indict traditional Hindu society.

There are glimpses of religious superstitions like Jayadev's mother's dedication of her right hand to Shiva for her son's long life, plan for Mohini's pleasing the goddess of birth, etc. Again, blind faith in astrology and palmistry is spotlighted here through the fate of Sudha and belief on the presence of all the eight signs of luck on Mohini's palm. All these are fabricated in the story of the novel to suggest the need for change.

Jayadev's Big House represents a miniature society full of stern discipline, iron tradition, orthodoxy and prohibitions like: prohibition of singing loudly by a woman, the tradition of using only the handloom saries, to keep customary hair style in all occasions, prohibition of the mistress of the house from moving out of the house on foot, the custom of segregation of men and women during meal time except on social occasions, the preservation of ancestral ideals even in the use of the bedstead, the necessity for Mohini's begetting a son for the continuation of the family tradition, the tradition of preserving the sanctity of 'Sati,' the customary act of alleviating the sufferings of the famine, etc.

Besides, there are other superstitions like—Heeralal's interpretation of the itching of his back as an omen of beating to be inflicted, exclusion of a widow from taking part in the reception of a new bride into the household, wearing of bamboo chip in the braided hair to ward off evil and to protect a woman's pregnancy, belief in a crocodile to be a reincarnation of a devout Brahmin and a Brahmin priest's objection to the removal of the hyacinth growing on the water where the crocodile lives, etc.

There are other traditional practices such as—the worship of tulsi plant, the service of professional puranic story-tellers, the ceremony of a sister's anointing brothers evoking tender fraternal feeling, a wife's sacrifice to tolerate even a co-wife, etc. All these references are made to suggest the need for a change.

Again, the impact of Gandhian thought is felt in the protagonist Jayadev's passionate involvement with constructive programmes in the village like campaigns against, superstition, caste system and exploitation of women.

Social reformation and reconstruction programmes are being taken up by a group of the village youngmen in collaboration with Jayadev and Mohini. First, they overthrow a village moneylender's plan to marry a very young girl as a fourth wife. The foreign returned doctor Harindra lives in Behula to work for social freedom. This rebel doctor has to defy a timeless social practice by marrying a Brahmin girl Sudha. Jayadev introduces an old man's second marriage only with a widow. He intends to abolish the evil system of early marriage and the fetters of caste and creed. He teaches people not to believe in false astrology.

Other social reforms made by the enlightened section of the people in the novel are: Mohini's father's mocking at the practice of consulting horoscopes in this age of microscopes, Heeralal's objection to wearing an amulet round his neck. Harindra's ridiculing the myth of the devout crocodile, etc. Mohini's father ridicules the custom of bride fasting on the marriage day. Heeralal proves the value of allopathic medicine by saving his own mother who cannot be cured by his father's 'ayurvedic' medicine. Setting up a dispensary and by filling up unnecessary ponds the young men try to eradicate mosquito menace.

There are also other varieties of freedom such as: freedom attained after completing some great works; economic freedom, individual freedom, etc. Many revolutionary activities are made to get this freedom by Mohini, Sudha and Harindra.

Music for Mohini delineates the conflict of the two sharply contrasted values of the old and the new which ultimately come to a synthesis and reconciliation. Two sets of characters represent the two values. The old Mother of Mohini, Jayadev's mother, Sudha's grandfather and Harindra's father represent old values while Jayadev, Harindra, Mohini, her father and Sudha represent new ideals and attitudes. But at last they come to a harmonious plane and they adjust themselves with one another.

The conflict of old and new and their adjustment are shown in the novel in Harindra's family. Harindra defeats his father's ayurvedic medicines with his allopathic medicines by curing his own mother who cannot be cured by his father. But at last reconciliation comes between the father and the son. Again, the novel shows a compromise between city life and village life in the characters and attitudes of Mohini and Rooplekha. City-bred Mohini leads her married life happily in the village while the village-bred Rooplekha leads her married life successfully in Calcutta.

The synthesis of asceticism and aestheticism is also highlighted in the novel. The marriage of ascetic Jayadev and aesthetic Mohini symbolises this synthesis. The synthesis of two contraries—thought and action, is also depicted through Jayadev's efforts of attaining social harmony and freedom. Besides, being a novel written after India's Independence *Music for Mohini* shows the social life and changes of the post-Independence period. Caste-system, a patent feature of Indian social life, is realistically portrayed. Moreover, the author portrays Jayadev's programme to exterminate the evil of early marriage, the system of untouchability, the ban on widow remarriage, the caste-barriers, etc.

Regarding the characterisation in the novel, Bhattacharya portrays his characters with an intimate knowledge of human nature. The characters of Mohini, Jayadev, Mother, Sudha and Heeralal play prominent roles in the novel. But among all the characters Mohini's character is more convincingly drawn. She is a connecting link with the several phases and various events and episodes that take place in the story. She is beautiful and has a cinematic face and a sensitive musical voice. She feels that life without love is like jasmine without scent. By becoming a trustee of an alien tradition she struggles to reshape her mental values. She thinks herself to be the incarnation of power, fate and pride. She has captivating power of narrating stories. She loves the ancient Hindu legends and lore. For sometime she suffers like a prisoner in the Big House for the sake of her barrenness. Ranjan, the boy, is introduced to bring out the tenderness and the mother instinct in her. Resigning to the inscrutable Fate she faces a lot of sufferings. Finally, Destiny comes to her rescue and makes her life a bed of roses.

Heeralal is sketched as a supporting character to Mohini upto the time of her marriage. But later he pales into insignificance. Mohini's father is sketched as a renowned professor of history having the quality of kindness towards humanity and specially towards the students. He thinks for Mohini's marriage, her adjustment and well-being in the new atmosphere.

Two outstanding characters in the novel are Old Mother and Jayadev's mother who have their orthodoxy in common but are sharply contrasted to each other. Old mother is gentle and is the symbol of an intermixture of orthodoxy and modernism. Believing in superstition she has fixed ideas and iron prejudice against modernism. In spite of her orthodoxical and superstitious nature she can be reconciled with modernism.

Contrary to Old Mother is Jayadev's mother who is rigid and uncompromising in her view and orthodox beliefs. Even when she is defeated by Jayadev at the end she does not change her views. She is aloof, alone, stern-willed and simple with singleness of purpose. Unlike Old Mother this adamant mother does not allow change.

The character of Jayadev is imperfectly sketched. He is not shown to be closely attached to his wife. The temple episode shows his moral change only but not his leadership and positive action. He is a strange mixture of Old and new. He likes harmony of cultures in India and has a dream to reorientate the values and patterns of Hindu life. He also wishes a harmonious blending of political and social liberty. He is an ascetic sacrificing his all for the happiness of the people. He seeks a source of inspiration from Mohini.

As opposed to the Mother Rooplekha is portrayed as a married sister of Jayadev. She tries to change her habits for her husband's sake. She is village-bred and city-wed. Moulding the life of Mohini to the new set-up she paves the way for an easy mental assimilation in Mohini.

The character of Sudha is sketched as a mere assembly of attitudes. The cruel and blind faith makes this faultless, fair and fragile girl an unfortunate one. Although her wounded ego makes her cruel she knows the goodness and affection and so she does not think of doing harm to Mohini.

Harindra's character plays its part in the later phase of the story. As opposed to his father, a Kaviraj, he practises in allopathic medicine. He argues that medicine knows no race or nationality. He emphasises to make use of the best of East and West to fight the disease. He possesses a social reformist zeal and decides to marry the Brahmin girl Sudha by defying a timeless social practice.

Of the minor characters, Bindu, Ganesh, Ranjan, Meera and barber woman may be mentioned for their respective parts in the minor incidents weaving the novel's texture. None of the characters is invested with full bloom. About the failure of portraying various relationships among the characters in a competent and convincing manner Dr. Chandrasekharan remarks:

> "*Music for Mohini* is a novel with rather restricted scope dealing with a limited area of life and experience.... The novel also does not present a large variety of characters. There is very little movement and action. On the whole it gives an impression of tenuity."[11]

These remarks from a kindly disposed critic amount to a denial of the art and vision required to write a novel.

Since Bhattacharya was influenced by Gandhi, Tagore and Steinbeck, his novel dealing with a social milieu, presents the entire picture of society but not individual's personal history. So Dr. Shyam M. Asnani gives the following significant remark:

> "The characters in these novels tend to be, therefore, types rather than individuals as is true of the nineteenth century socio-political novels of England."[12]

Very clearly then, Bhattacharya's failure lies in his inability to see that ideas alone do not make art. As regards idea, these too are the common places of Indian nationalism.

One of the remarkable aspects of the novel, however, is the importance of woman characters. The writer presents their various roles as: mother and companion (represented by Old Mother and Mother; and Mohini), mother of seven-fold Bliss (Mohini), wife and beloved with subdued murmurings and unspoken demands (Mohini), reflection of mother India (Mohini), connecting culture with culture (Mohini and Rooplekha), harassing mother-in-law (Jayadev's mother and Old Mother), widow (Sudha), etc.

Music for Mohini has a well-constructed plot, but the novelist's artistic imagination is not sufficiently kindled, so that the story ends on a quiet and drab note. Once again we quote Chandrasekharan:

> "There is much in the novel to entertain, to delight and even to provoke. The music we hear however, is only the soft and subdued melody of flute and not the varied harmony of a rich Orchestra."[13]

This is, of course, an example of the critical voice subdued by kindness. The critic means to say that the novel does not offer the rich fare expected of a work of fiction.

Regarding the question of style, Bhattacharya uses in this novel literal translations of Bengali proverbs like: "You may be digging a canal from the river to the housedoor and inviting a crocodile" (*Music for Mohini,* New Delhi: Orient Paperback,

1952, 53), "The tail of a cow and the tongue of a rustic never cease wagging," (*Music for Mohini,* New Delhi: Orient Paperback, 1952, 70), "Why expect our girl to be like them? How can a plum tree grow pears?" (*Music for Mohini,* New Delhi: Orient Paperback, 1952, 129). Besides, there are many illiterate Bengali expressions in the novel which are obviously not English like: "a bareman height" when referring to the height of the sun in the sky (*Music for Mohini,* New Delhi: Orient Paperback, 1952, 129). Changing of the normal structure and rhythm of English sentences like: "who more proud than I on this..." (*Music for Mohini,* New Delhi: Orient Paperback, 1952, 88), instead of "who is more proud...etc.," the use of non-technical terms in place of complex ones like: "the wonder ray" for the "X-ray" (*Music for Mohini,* New Delhi: Orient Paperback, 1952, 147), the use of ironical English names like: "Whiteleather, Miss Stiff and Miss Coffin, etc. are some of the items that are apt to repel a reader.

To sum up: *Music for Mohini* is a successful novel working on the theme of harmonisation of many contrastive aspects of human life in the Hindu society of post-Independence India. It is not merely a catalogue of the social evils of Hindu India to delight a Western audience but a portrait of the contrasting values of the old and the new in sharp conflict with each other and ending in a reconciliation and synthesis of the two.

3. *He Who Rides a Tiger*

Published in 1954, *He Who Rides a Tiger* is Bhabani Bhattacharya's third novel based on the ancient saying—"He who rides a tiger cannot dismount." But the hero, Kalo, has the courage to dismount from the tiger in the hour of crisis. He can face the situation and identify himself with the society. The novel narrates an individual's history and his ultimate liberation of spirit.

This novel has a common background with *So Many Hungers*! The Indian Freedom struggle and the Bengal Famine of 1943 are the two major themes dealt with in both of them. But the treatment of the theme and the final effect aimed at and produced make them different. Dr. K.R. Chandrasekharan aptly states:

> "While the earlier novel focuses attention on the national movement and Bengal's travail and their cataclysmic effect on the teeming millions of people, the later novel is more concerned with the history of one mind or at the most of two or three minds."[14]

In fact, this novel is by no means a mere replica of the earlier one, for, it attacks the social reality of caste and class system and its dehumanising effect on the growth of individual character. It is a moral fable of human depravity and degradation to get out of the moral morass of fraud and falsehood. The following analysis of the story of the novel will show that this novel has not only a change of focus of attention but also a new approach to the theme of the earlier novel.

The story begins with the depiction of the happy life of Kalo, a dark-skinned, self-competent, industrious and ambitious blacksmith of Jharna town. His pretty wife dies in childbirth but the baby daughter is named Chandralekha. The baby grows up into a girl by displaying intelligence and inheriting her mother's good looks. She is sent to the local English Convent School and in the final year in the school she wins a gold medal for writing the best essay in all State Essay Writing Competition. Kalo takes the medal out of its casket everyday and spends sometime fondly looking at it. He adores her and spends his time happily in the memory of his dead wife.

While spending life happily with the mutual affection between the father and the daughter the Bengal Famine strikes the land. The tillers of the soil are reduced to starvation. Weavers and other tradesmen sell their implements and are forced to leave for Calcutta in search of food and work. With an aching heart Kalo also leaves for Calcutta leaving behind his daughter in the care of an old aunt.

While travelling on the foot-board of a train Kalo steals some bananas from a carriage. He is arrested and sentenced to three months' imprisonment by the harsh magistrate who taunts Kalo: "Why did you have to live?" In the prison Kalo meets B-10 (Bikash Mukherjee), a Quit India political prisoner. B-10 disillusions Kalo about his honest living in the cruel city. He advises him to retaliate against society by faking a miracle and by befooling people making them worship his bogus image.

When released from the jail, hunger compels Kalo to remove corpses of destitutes for a meagre wage. Soon he turns into a pimp for a group of brothels managed by one Rajani Bose. One night he hears the protesting cries of a girl from a nearby room. He rushes into that room to find to his horror that the girl is his own daughter. He saves her before her honour is stained. But he becomes bitter in his heart against the corrupt society. Remembering what B-10 said in the jail: "We are the scum of the earth. They hit us where it hurts badly—in the belly. We've got to hit back,"[15] he resolves to take revenge upon this society.

Kalo performs the miracle by making a phallic image of Shiva rise out of the soil under an old banyan tree. A temple is created and inaugurated on the hallowed spot. Money is showered by black-marketeers and profiteers. By wearing a nine stranded sacred thread and a saffron robe Kalo metamorphoses into Mangal Adhikari, the prosperous priest of the temple. Chandralekha also becomes an ascetic girl. A pujari is appointed to perform the ritual worship. A Board of Trustees is constituted to manage the temple. The rich merchants like Sir Abalabandhu and stock brokers like Motichand become Mangal Adhikari's devotees and even the magistrate, who had sent Kalo to jail for stealing bananas, comes to the temple and touches his feet—the knight of the satire.

Taking B-10 to his residence on the day of his release from the jail Kalo offers him a share of the temple income. But B-10 turns down the offer since his plan for future is different. He prophesies Kalo's tiredness of the game in due course. Explaining Kalo's nature Chandrasekharan remarks:

> "Kalo has over-reached himself and while deceiving the society that he hates, he is also deceiving himself. He has more or less persuaded himself that he is a Brahmin. Truly he is now riding a tiger and cannot get down from its back. He is playing the Brahminic role with gusto."[16]

Though outwardly happy he suffers from depression in his new role. He is troubled when the coolies and rickshaw pullers, beggars and cripples and destitutes sacrifice their hard earned money on his fake god. He sees Lekha feeling the temple to be a "gilded-cage" spreading corruption inside her. He also knows of the love between Lekha and Biten. Kalo, however, feels that after having mounted the tiger's back once, there is no way out for him but to ride on.

Taking an old destitute blacksmith, Viswanath, into his house, Kalo gives him the work of a gardener. He also takes into his home a destitute boy and gives him the Brahminic name Obhijit. Lekha is very fond of the boy and treats him as her younger brother. Biswanath steals the milk used for Shiva's ritual bath and distributes it to the destitute children in the neighbourhood. Touched by the humanity of the gesture Mangal Adhikari supports Viswanath. But this is considered as sacrilege and the trustees paying for the milk through endowments create an uproar, which is subsided finally by adopting the custom of feeding the hungry children with the sanctified milk. Mangal Adhikari wants B-10 to wear a sacred thread and call himself a Brahmin to marry Lekha without shocking public opinion. But B-10 refuses because he knows that Lekha feels hatred of him for his act of love-making one day while they are alone. And noticing this Biten (B-10) leaves them till near the end of the story. He has awakened the woman in her. She finds her father losing his original simplicity and rectitude and she is unhappy for this and about the hypocritical part she too has been playing so far. The predicament suggested in the title reappears; it is difficult for them to dismount from the tiger's back; although the metaphor is a bit too bold.

Lekha is so much venerated in the temple that the people want to deify her as the Mother of seven fold Bliss. She agrees to this. But Motichand proposes to marry Lekha as his fourth wife. This makes Kalo and Lekha scandalised. But on second thought Lekha who knows that her father will not quit the game, decides to marry him, with a sacrificial spirit of course.

The crisis comes when Kalo realises that Lekha is going to ruin herself for his sake by marrying Motichand, the old shark with his cast off wives. He sees his moral fall and deception of his own inner-self instead of his enemies with his idea of taking revenge on society.

So full of indignation he decides to take a bold step. When he is asked to make a speech before the crowd assembled for the installation of Lekha as Mother of sevenfold Bliss, he stuns everyone by revealing his true identity and by narrating all about the fake miracle of raising a Shiva image. This revelation produces different reactions among the audience. Enraged by this humiliation some Brahmins want to beat him up while some suggest legal action. But the crowd of the poor, the low-caste and the destitute who outnumbered the Brahmins are happy that one of their class has made the mighty ones eat dirt and they shouts: "Victory to our brother."

In the meantime Kalo has learnt that Biten is a Brahmin by birth whose real name is Bikash Mukherji. Biten is present there and he congratulates Kalo by telling him "Your story will be a legend of freedom." Unable to contain her exultation Lekha says to her father: "Baba, after this, whatever happens to us, wherever we go, we can never again be unhappy or defeated." Then Kalo and Lekha walk out of the temple to go back to their former way of life seeking the peace which is the fruit of being true to one's own self.

Thus in this novel the novelist shows the wonderful spirit of the poor folk, who instead of committing suicide in their desperate state, believe in the preservation of life in dignified manner. The end of the novel showing Lekha and her father's undaunted spirit to lead a new life in future free from all vices justifies the novelist's bright view of life.

With an ingenious, inventive and mechanical plot based on the Bengal Famine this novel deals with a hero who is a bogus holy man. So there is a vicious satirical twist in him while the theme is intricate. Besides, this novel catches glimpses of Gandhian protest against social evils.

The theme presents many aspects like—the political, social, religious and economic aspect, etc. The political situation in the country of pre-Independence period is shown by the reference to the Quit India Movement, imprisonment of people for loving their motherland, the relentless attitude of the British soldiers to the spectacle of hunger and suffering, etc. By referring to a former political prisoner, Biten, we are shown the involvement of people in the struggle for political emancipation.

The novel also deals with the theme of social freedom. Casteism is seriously protested through the inset story of Biten. Biten's sister, Purnima is hastily given away in marriage to an elderly widower. But her parents soon discover her love-relation with Basav, a man of lower caste. Her unhappy life leads her to commit suicide and Basav taunts Biten about this. Biten, thereby, renounces his Brahminhood throwing away his sacred thread and promising never more to speak about his caste. This is why he refuses to disclose his caste when Kalo questions him about it. So he takes the risk of losing the girl whom he loves.

There are other references to the denunciation of caste-tyranny. Lekha's education criticised by both the high-caste and low-caste people of Jharna shows the root of caste-system and the difficulty to eradicate it. Kalo's rebuking the Kamar Viswanath for touching and polluting him while he is wearing the Brahmin mask temporarily exposes the arrogance of the upper class people. The pujari's wife's treatment of the boy Obhijit also exemplifies caste tyranny.

Although Biten's repudiation of caste is depicted affectively as a protest against caste system, Kalo also is portrayed as championing the social freedom. By performing a miracle he becomes an exponent of freedom. At last Biten proclaims Kalo to be a great exponent of social freedom:

> "You have triumphed over those others and over yourself. What you have done just now will steel the spirit of hundred and thousands of us. Your story will be a legend of freedom, a legend to inspire and awaken."[17]

In addition to the social freedom the novelist also deals with the individual freedom. That man needs individual freedom is shown by the decision of Lekha to marry Motichand who has already three wives. To achieve personal freedom which she loses as daughter of the priest, she prepares to marry Motichand. Kalo's act of disclosing his real identity to be a blacksmith and not a Brahmin is also urged by his desire for personal freedom. So he abandons the mask of Brahmin to show his real identity to lead an independent personal life.

In *He Who Rides a Tiger* the novelist discusses the religious aspect of the Hindu society. There are certain references to Hindu religion as practised by the people of the country like the people's eager expectation of Kalo's promised miracle, offering of money and materials for the construction of false temple, etc. In fact, the novelist exposes the wicked practices of the hollow religion. Thus in the story religion seems to have lost its pristine glory and forgotten its ethical values. It is turned into a spiritual trade where people try to bury spiritual merit in exchange for merchandise.

The economic aspect concerning hunger for food consequent on the Bengal Famine of 1943 forms the prominent part of the novel's background. Kalo's story of protest shows us the ordeals of countless destitutes and their hunger which instill in them the courage to rebel in an emphatic way. The destitute Viswanath's joining the procession of starving men raising the cries: "Food for all," "work for all" and "jail for the rice profiteers,"[18] exemplifies such spirit. In fact, the novel highlights the protest against the evil of exploitation of the have-nots by the haves.

Besides this hunger for food, man's unending hunger for worldly pleasures, material possessions and economic profits is also dealt with in this novel. People hoard great quantity of food for increasing their possession and pleasure. The theme of hunger signifies the title of the novel *He Who Rides a Tiger.* Riding on the tiger implies man's quest for riding on hunger. Hunger is ferocious and is killing man as a tiger does. Kalo and Lekha, the two central characters, suffer from hunger losing their all on account of it. So they decide to ride the tiger of hunger to eke out their living.

The novel also attempts at removing caste and class barriers to achieve their synthesis—synthesis of Kamar and Brahmin class of people. The idea of synthesis of high and low castes is seen in Lekha's intention to marry Motichand and also in Biten's proposal to marry Lekha.

Recording the milieu of the Bengal Famine of 1943 and the Quit India Movement the novel expresses many brutal social realities like—throwing of innocent girls to brothels, imprisonment of men for minor lapses and inhuman torture of convict in prison. These things lead Kalo, Lekha and Biten to fight against cruel social forces. Thus the novel depicts their success in hitting back the rich and the high caste Hindus.

Regarding characterisation in the novel it is clear that the story of the novel concentrates on Kalo and Lekha. Kalo's name is meaningful and suggestive and it is in keeping with his role as *Kamar,* the blacksmith. Taking the role of a Brahmin he easily acquires wealth and fame which he can use whenever required. Now there is a conflict in his mind between comfort, power and prestige on one side and desire to be true to himself on the other.

Finally, he is able to kill the tiger of deceit when he earns his moral strength to be himself. During his tiger-ride his personality is disintegrated but slaying the tiger ultimately he can reintegrate it by winning spiritual victory and spiritual liberation.

Chandralekha is true to her name in features and actions. Like a digit of the moon that waxes and wanes, her temperament also changes from mildness to seriousness as occasion demands. Her character is steady. She feels greater discomfort in riding the tiger than her father and so she has less inclination to ride it furthermore. Her acceptance of the position into which she is forced is passive.

Lekha is an image of suffering who is subjected to traditional restraints. The caste restrictions and her role of priestess in the temple add to the suffering of this motherless girl. But she bears them silently. She is saved in time from a brothel by her father. She has the role of an ideal companion woman in the development of Kalo's activities. She works as redeemer by getting rid of the burden of falsehood—the imposture as a Brahmin and as a Goddess and by desiring to link her life with Biten for the emancipation of the downtrodden people. She is deified as the Mother of seven-fold Bliss and portrayed as an embodiment of succour and sacrifice. Though deified, Lekha has the primal urge of woman and she wants to be a human being. She is sensitive, introspective and intriguing.

Biten is an important character. This name is a funny variation of B-10. His attitude is biting on the ways of society and so he suggests an equally biting reaction. Rajani is the anchor of hope while Sir Abalabandhu meaning the friend of helpless is a negation of his own name in action. Bhattacharya, thus, portrays all his characters giving them suggestive, meaningful and significant names and they play their part successfully in the development of the story. In fine, he is able to invent new events and characters even though the theme is the same as in the earlier novels.

Regarding the style and diction it is seen that the novel is written in a light veined style, full of pleasantries and exaggerations and spiced with irony and a sense of humour.

Bhattacharya uses free expression of Bengali proverbs. But his literal translations are more consistent and smooth in this novel as compared to those of his earlier novels. The use of flashback or recapitulation technique of narration and the habit of using significant expressions recurrently make the style impressive and attractive. But the use of odd adjectival forms with the suffix *ful* and the use of strange diminutives with the suffix *ling* make the diction indistinct and distorted.

4. *A Goddess Named Gold*

Bhabani Bhattacharya's fourth novel *A Goddess Named Gold* was published in 1960. This novel highlights the post-Independence national consciousness. An analysis of the novel will show how the present freedom of ours is not that which Gandhi sought; it is only a privilege for a handful of wealthy men. Specifically, the novel deals with the theme of the economic freedom of the hungry masses. The novel is a women's novel because in it the liberation of the country from the clutches of the Sethji is accomplished by women alone.

Opening actually a hundred days before Indian Independence Day in a village called Sonamitti, symbolic of earth yielding gold, we are introduced to a group of six women, *the Cowhouse Five,* a name derived from their holding of daily meetings in the unused cow-shed in the house of Lakshmi who is also one of them. These women are all ardent nationalists imprisoned for participation in the Quit India Movement. Lakshmi's husband Seth Samsundar is a cloth merchant and moneylender controlling the market in the group of five villages to which Sonamitti belongs. Trained in Gandhian Satyagraha *the Cowhouse Five* decides to launch a strike against the Seth demanding fair prices for cloth.

The theme of the novel runs between Samsundar and the heroine Meera, a girl of sixteen living with her patriotic grandmother. At the age of eleven she joined the Quit India Movement, for which she was arrested. She suggests a protest march of the village women to the Seth's shop demanding a hundred saries at fair price. Another suggests that they should strip themselves naked and march through the streets to arouse the conscience of the Sethji if he does not relent. *The Cowhouse Five* approves these suggestions. As planned already, the demonstration takes place at midday. Meera joins it after her acts of rescuing Nago, the only son of Sethji and Lakshmi's, who falls into a well while flying a kite. But the demonstration and even Meera's threat to strip herself do not frighten the Seth. But when his wife Lakshmi begins to divest herself of her sari, he relents and sells out two bundles of saries on the spot.

The Seth desires to contest the election to the District Board for which he requires to win the good will of the people of the village. So the sale of the saries is not an act of kindness but an investment for his winning vote. He organises a procession of school boys who shout "Vote for Samsundar." He arranges a free cinema show where all the women are to be kept out. This depresses the women and they think out to thwart his purpose.

In the meantime Meera's grandfather Atmaram, who is a wandering minstrel, appears on the scene. He gives Meera an amulet and tells her that if she does an act of kindness all the copper on her body will turn into gold. Lakshmi shows her gratitude to Meera by offering a gold ring for saving her child Nago but she refuses. As suggested by the minstrel Lakshmi replaces the copper ring on Meera's finger with a gold one when she is asleep. Meera knows nothing about it. When Meera is at the shop of the Seth, the Seth and she herself discover that the ring on her finger is of gold and both are convinced of the amulet's power.

Afterwards the Seth enters into a business contract with Meera on a fifty-fifty basis. Now Meera's body is wrapped with copper ornaments. Her waist ornaments have given a bulge to her abdomen and her grandmother, misunderstanding the situation, thinks that Meera is pregnant.

Now the Seth has to make experiments for making the amulet function. The novelist here shows Meera's motivated acts of kindness, combined by the Seth one after another. These are parodies of those spontaneous acts of compassion performed by Meera like her rescuing Nago from a well, her saving a man bitten by a cobra and her touching kindness to the cow, Soondri, suffering from labour pain and finally dying of it and her giving sweets to Buddhu who hungrily licks the leaves thrown by customers in front of the sweet shop.

As a calculated act of kindness, the Seth arranges to distribute sweets to all the urchins employed by him for his election campaign. The boys receive the sweets and yell "Vote—for Meera Bai!" The Seth's investment in sweets has been lost and the plan is a failure. This episode objectifies Bhattacharya's comic vision and skilful use of irony of situation.

Another act of kindness devised by the Seth is the cruel caricature of the incident in which Meera saved the Seth's son. The Seth tempts the poor boy, Buddhu, to fly kites near the well. He summons Meera to his shop. Meanwhile he engages his assistant Bulaki Rao to contrive everything. While Meera and the Seth are talking in the shop Bulaki Rao announces that Buddhu falls into the well. The Seth asks Meera to descend into the well and she inclines to do it. But in the moment Sohanlal, the Seth's driver and Meera's lover arrives on the scene. He tries to descend into the well instead of Meera. The Seth is angry because his plan has failed. He asks Bulaki Rao to bring out the boy who has been asked to hide himself in the latrine. This episode signifies Bhattacharya's successful use of irony for comic effect. This frantic experiment with act of kindness which, in fact, is a selfish act, is a paradigm of irony of situation.

Another plan made by the Seth is his eviction of the Old father and his family from their ancestral home. He makes the situation expecting that Meera will offer money to the victims to redeem their mortgaged house. But the old man knows that it is the Seth's money and so he refuses to accept it. He, along with his family, therefore, leaves the house and the village forever.

As a last attempt to make the amulet function the Seth persuades a drunkard and a prostitute to marry in the "presence" of Meera. But the marriage is going to be a complete failure as the drunkard demands money from the Seth to buy liquor while the bride continues her trade upto the scheduled hour of the marriage. Now Meera wakes up herself. She takes off all the copper ornaments and throws them on the ground. She then goes away. But the Seth has his hope still.

On the eve of the Independence Day the minstrel arrives in the village. He tells Meera about her would be marriage to a rich man in Delhi after becoming the goddess of plenty. Meera is annoyed at this insinuation because her craving for gold is only to do good to others. Outraged at this insinuation she wrenches the amulet from her arm and casts it into the river.

The minstrel tells the people, thronged under a banyan tree for celebration of Independence Day, that the freedom which they are celebrating is the real touchstone. The villagers decide to use their newly won freedom in the right way by electing the minstrel to the District Board. The Seth does not show any external sigh of disappointment while the minstrel has a reasonable chance of winning the election as his wife is not likely to be his rival. With this decision of the villagers the novel ends.

The novel may be interpreted as one dealing with the themes of freedom, hunger, affirmation and synthesis. The heroine Meera lives amid the tragic circumstances of life. But she bears an affirmative attitude towards life. Likewise, the profiteer Seth is usually seen cheerful and hopeful in spite of the failure of all his plans. The novel also deals with the hunger for gold, miracle and spiritual experience. As the title denotes, the novel primarily dwells on man's hunger for gold, power and possessions.

The novelist also touches upon the theme of synthesis of two contrastive characters—the Seth and his wife. Lakshmi who is a good and patriotic minded wife lives with her wicked and unpatriotic minded husband Seth happily. Again, synthesis of the tragic and comic, is seen in Atmaram, the minstrel who is composer and singer of tragic and comic songs. The synthesis of the real and unreal is seen in the Seth and Meera.

The theme of freedom is dealt with vividly in this novel. The novel depicts Indian villagers including women involved in the freedom movement. The feminist organisation, *the Cowhouse Five* with its members—Munni, Champa, Meera, Subhadri, Sohagi and Lakshmi—plays a great role in the freedom movement. The Quit India Movement of 1942 is referred to in the speech of Lakshmi addressed to Meera and others.

The novel also depicts women's role to secure economic freedom through the Gandhian way of Satyaraha and procession. It shows village women launching a movement against the Seth to bring down prices of essential commodities under the leadership of Meera, the image of woman power.

Another aspect of freedom dealt with in the novel is social freedom. The novelist aims at liberating the innocent and good villagers from superstitions. In fact, the novel expresses the novelist's lofty concept of freedom through the actions and words of the minstrel. At the end of the novel he asserts that freedom is the touchstone with the help of which people can perform great miracles provided they do acts of faith.

One of the remarkable features of the novel is its political satire. The novelist satirises the self-styled pseudo-politicians who wear Gandhi cap, which is supposed to wash off all the sins committed by the wearer. The novelist also satirises the election methods. For winning the election the Seth spends a lot of money and employs all sorts of stunts to buy votes. These are no doubt aimed at satirising the post-independence political culture of corruption.

There are references to people's belief in the ancient epics, astrology, ghosts, devils, amulets, marvelous legend of the talking goat, the evils of dowry, bribery and corrupt practices, the extravagance of the Indians during marriage and other ceremonies, cruelty of moneylenders, scientific invention of penicillin, adoration of the cow, ceiling on all holdings including land, the lure of gold by all, etc. To sum up: *A Goddess Named Gold* gives a picture of India in its sordid reality and ominous future even though individual growth is not lacking.

In this novel Bhattacharya has introduced the device of allegory and symbolism. The title of the novel itself is highly symbolic obviously, gold and Goddess are the two important symbols around which the whole thematic structure of the novel centres. Meera is the symbol of the goddess *i.e.* Mother India possessed by gold. The village Sonamitti has symbolically two meanings: the danger of gold becoming clay if our people are greedy and selfish and the chance of clay becoming gold provided our people are good and pure in mind. The amulet itself stands symbolically for freedom and hope. This double suggestiveness gives to the novel a great thematic interest.

The novel shows important characters symbolically standing for certain values and ideas. The Seth symbolises the blind principle of capitalism and Meera symbolises the compassionate mother India but the minstrel is a symbolic voice working against the Seth's powers and as a patriotic nationalist he appears as the voice of Mahatma Gandhi.

Two more symbols employed by the novelist are "a spider's catching a red ant symbolising the Seth's acts of trapping and destroying gullible victims and a snake devouring half a frog symbolising the Seth's act of expulsion of Old Father from his original house."

There are many improbable episodes and events in the plot of the novel. Some of these incredible acts are: villagers' credulity in the amulet's power, the prostitute's plying of her trade upto the scheduled minute of her marriage, leaving the site of cinema show for fear of monkey's attack, fear of ghosts, eviction of Old Father for his debt to the Seth, etc.

As is characteristic and natural, the narrative design of Bhattacharya's novel has a historical and contemporary context which is rooted in character and situation. But this novel, an allegory of greed for material wealth is less concerned with clash of values. Bhattacharya depicts skilfully and with acuteness the characters and episode in the novel. The reader's attention is focused on the trinity—Seth Samsundar, his wife Lakshmi and Meera. In the sub-plot Meera and Sohanlal play a pretty part. The minstrel, absent or present, pervasively influences on all events of the novel.

One of the marked features of the novel is its successful characterisation. Meera, the heroine of the novel is sketched as a combination of intelligence, generosity, patriotism and stupidity. Bhattacharya delves deeply into Meera's increasingly troubled mind as she becomes the unconscious instrument for evil and the conscious instrument for good. She has a strong will and nothing can shake her out of her will. She is brave and faithful. Her motto is to use "old means for new ends." She has no greed for gold. Failure does not deem her hopes. She is portrayed in various roles: Earth Mother Goddess, redeemer, Mother of seven-fold Bliss and newly freed Mother India.

Seth Samsundar is sketched as a proud and extortionist cloth merchant, parading about in his gaudy English bathrobe and parasol, thrice, the gullible victim of following superstitions, get rich quick schemes. In fact, his character reminds us of Shakespeare's Shylock and Marlowe's Barabas. His character is nothing but a caricature of the greedy exploiter.

A device Bhattacharya commonly uses in characterisation is that of parallelism or contrast. Seth Samsundar's wife Lakshmi is presented as a contrast to her husband in her dealings with men and matters. She joins her friends in launching a movement against her own husband to bring down the price of clothes.

The character of the minstrel is successfully carved out in the novel. He is the *deus ex-machina.* He is Meera's grandfather, a wandering minstrel visiting his family and village only occasionally and about whose wanderings and activities little is known. He can compose wonderful songs and he is mysterious man surrounded by an aura of greatness. Because of his previous birth as Atmaram, a disciple of a great Himalayan sage to whom he goes by a kind of instinct and who also recognises him as Atmaram, he is known as Atmaram. But really he is nameless. He tells stories which are believed by the villagers except his own wife. He is an unusual character and a veiled representation of Mahatma Gandhi, a homeless wanderer mixing with large crowds, a man among men but deified by a grateful and admiring people everywhere. His character is a contrast to that of Seth Samsundar. A very benign presence that he is, he is worshipped and admired by his people.

Bhattacharya also projects the character of Sohanlal, Meera's beau as a sensible ex-soldier and reputed city swank. But he is sketched as a one dimensional re-incarnation of B-10 from *He Who Rides a Tiger*. The novelist successfully portrays Meera's grandmother. She is the only sufficient complement to Meera with her zeal of freedom fighter and a marvellous sense of humour, kindly instincts, and pragmatic insights.

A Goddess Named Gold, as is typical of Bhattacharyan novels, is full of literal translation of Bengali proverbs and Indian phrases, coining of new idioms having no counterparts in English, use of unidiomatic English, metaphors, similes, irony and humour are important features of style in this novel. On a number of occasions, the novelist uses the Gandhian expression: "to wipe every tear from every eye." The novelist also uses diminutives and abusive epithets along with his calling the name of the implement for a workman and the name of the article for a merchant and characteristically enough he packs so many of the social ideas, many of them common-place, that the novel reads more like a social commentary than fiction. Still the foreign reader is likely to be interested because of its seeming revelation of the superstitions and materialistic Hindu society. There is an inevitable amount of sexual titillation also, with Meera threatening to strip and the rich merchant's wife, Godiva—like, following suit. Critics may someday come to a consensus about the artistic worth of Bhattacharya's characterisation.

5. *Shadow from Lakakh*

Bhabani Bhattacharya's fifth novel *Shadow from Ladakh* was published in the year 1966. This novel brought the Sahitya Akademi Award for 1967 to the novelist. It has been suggested that the title is based on the popular proverb "coming events cast their shadows before them." The novel is not against the menacing background of the Chinese aggression in 1962. The shadow of the military encounter with the unexpected enemy at Ladakh is cast everywhere. The theme registers the conflict of ideologies during this critical juncture of Indian history. The love between Bhashkar Roy and Sumita, initially opposed by lifestyle and ideology, is an allegory of how such conflicts of ideologies can be solved.

It is evident that Bhattacharya is aiming at a vision of social regeneration in India by synthesising Gandhism and Nehruism. A full analysis of the novel will show a synthesis of the spinning wheel and the spindle. Another synthesis is of Gandhiji's asceticism and Tagore's aestheticism.

While the whole action of the novel is based on the shadow cast by the Chinese peril, many of the characters are shadows too chasing other shadows. Satyajit and Gandhigram are shadows of Gandhi and Sevagram. Similarly, Bhashkar and steel town are shadows of Nehru and his dream edifices of industry. The question whether there is possibility for co-existence between Steel town's blast furnaces and Gandhigram's spinning wheels—produces another question whether there is possibility of peaceful co-existence between Mao's armour plated expansionist absolutist China and Nehru's democratic socialist federal republic. Mao's China trying to annex India is the real thing and steel town trying to swallow up Gandhigram is the parallel, the shadow from Ladakh.

The novel is an attempt to find out the meeting point of the Gandhian social ethics and the tremendous forces of science and technology. Bhattacharya made the Gandhian principle of simple living and high thinking" a mode of life, an ideal to live by. The novel deals with the conflict of values and ultimate triumph of the Gandhian principle. Two ways of life, industrial and rural, are contrasted in this novel. The novelist backs Satyajit who is a miniature Gandhi. However, he is equally aware of the need of India's industrialisation in view of the growing population as well as the external threat. Here the novelist is ambivalent.

Taking extreme positions Bhashkar and Satyajit lead two opposing ways of life never to be harmonised. But Sumita, moulded in Satyajit's image and planning to marry Bhashkar, will be the meeting point of the two opposing ways.

The conflict of ideologies is symbolised by the clash between Gandhigram and Steeltown. Satyajit is the leader of Gandhigram. He is a true Gandhian in an austere life and ascetic thought and a true Tagorean in his educational and aesthetic ideals. He patterns the village after the Gandhian values. He was married at Santiniketan to beautiful Suruchi, a woman of great vitality, and brought up on the refinements of Tagorean culture. The couple has a lovely and worthy daughter, Sumita who is carefully trained by her father.

But soon Satyajit faces a conflict in his domestic life as Suruchi is against his austerities and as Sumita loves for the Tagorean aestheticism. Satyajit forces sexual abstinence on Suruchi but she and Sumita believe in his ideal and dedicate themselves to a life of stern austerities. Thus Satyajit becomes a disciplined Gandhian applying the principles of Gandhian economics and ethics in the regulation of the life of Gandhigram and the conduct of his own life.

While India, symbolised by Gandhigram, is on the path of progress, a testing time comes with the Chinese aggression. India Government's one point of view is to meet strength with strength but Satyajit is against this view. As he is a firm believer in non-violence he plans for a Peace March to Ladakh in the hope that he would touch the hearts of the Chinese and make them give up their aggressive intentions. He believes in the idea of facing hatred with love.

At all the three levels—economic, personal and international, Satyajitism faces antagonistic forces. The idyllic life of Gandhigram is disturbed and Gandhian economics is threatened by the new cry of industrialisation specially when Steeltown with its heavy machines and blast furnaces springs up in the vicinity of Gandhigram. With the shadow from Ladakh hovering over the whole country steel comes to acquire a greater significance. It stands as the symbol of India's freedom since it is the core of all armament. The American trained young Chief Engineer Bhashkar Roy is the moving force behind Steeltown. He represents a three dimensional opposition to Satyajit and Satyajitism. His American education makes him believe in steel standing for mass production to cope with the growing population of India, providing a shield to protect the infant democracy against all enemies.

Bhashkar wants to expand his steeltown factory which will result in annexing Gandhigram. Devoting to his work he spares no pains in labouring to speed up the production "to make four hundred million lives a little more livable." Thus, the two completely dedicated men, Satyajit and Bhashkar, are brought to polar opposition. The board of Directors of the Unit of Lohapur Steel Company finally approves his scheme of expansion. Even Nehru's Government gives him permission for this expansion. This Chinese invasion justifies Bhashkar's standpoint and gives added urgency in executing his plan.

Bhashkar knows that Satyajit is the real obstacle to his plan for he is a man with a soul force ready to match any political or legal pressure. On the other hand, Satyajit is rocked by two burning problems—the peril of the country from China's attack and the peril of Gandhigram being swallowed up by Steeltown.

Of the two burning problems—China's attack on India, the national cause, gets priority with Satyajit and he puts forward a proposal to the Government for a Peace Mission to Ladakh. But the Government rejects his proposal. At last the proposal is accepted with a slight modification. But the Chinese order ceasefire and withdraw their forces unilaterally. Thus, ends the nation's problem for the time being but leaves the conflict in the nation's policy unresolved.

Satyajit returns to Gandhigram and he is ready to resist against Steeltown's expansion by undertaking a fast unto death. He announces it in the language that Gandhi used on the occasion of one of his crucial fasts in the past.

Bhashkar is intelligent enough to understand the value of non-violence and he keeps reverence for Satyajit. He has ordered the construction of Meadow House and has set up a club there half way between Steeltown and Gandhigram to win Gandhigram over to his side by encouraging the free mixing of the sexes of both the places in the club. He witnesses his first success when Jhanak, a girl of Gandhigram, revolts against its philosophy of anti-life. Then many of the people of Gandhigram including Sumita begin to take interest in the activities of the Meadow House. No longer is there an impenetrable barrier between the two worlds.

When Sumita learns Bhashkar's designs against Gandhigram, she is repelled by his deceit and she goes to Delhi to support her father there. Her company with Nandini, the niece of Bireswar and her visits to historical monuments of Delhi, its restaurants and clubs, make her see life in its full splendour and heighten her awareness of her womanhood. After her return to Gandhigram she has been attracted to the westernised culture of steeltown and to Bhashkar, the living symbol of this culture.

Bhashkar's falling in love with Sumita brings a synthesis or compromise of the two different ideologies. Bhashkar's attitude to Satyajit and his ideal undergoes a change. He ultimately decides not to annex Gandhigram in the way he proposed. Bhashkar himself leads a procession of workmen from steeltown to Gandhigram to announce the victory of Satyajit. Thus the crisis of the novel is resolved. Satyajit gains Gandhigram at the cost of Sumita who is at last free from the curse of anti-life and asceticism.

Thus, the two ideologies are to co-exist and Bhashkar's marriage to Sumita is the marriage of steeltown to Gandhigram. While Bhashkar has changed his ideal and attitude to the village, Satyajit also has changed a lot. Then comes the end of the issue which is described by G.P. Sarma as:

> "A happy combination of Gandhi, Nehru and Tagore together."[19]

Bhattacharya is concerned with the future of India, her social, religious, economic and political regeneration. So the story shows that in the contemporary context, neither Gandhism nor Nehruism can be alone the national ideal; only a harmonious combination of the two would be an answer to the problems facing the nation today.

The novelist uses parallelism and contrast too mechanically in this novel. Satyajit is contrasted with Bhashkar and to a lesser extent with Bireswar. Similarly, Sumita is contrasted with Rupa and Jhanak. The novelist makes Suruchi move from freshness and spontaneity towards asceticism while Sumita moves a counter-movement from asceticism towards fullness of life and freedom. But a compromise and equilibrium form the message of the final analysis.

Bhattacharya highlights the contrast between urban and rural life. Through Bhashkar Roy and Satyajit he shows how modern sophisticated civilisation enchroaches upon the simple and unassuming lives of the poor villagers.

The novelist makes Gandhigram a microcosm of India. In the novel he shows that the Gandhian economics and ethics are true everywhere and at any time. He also hopes that even China can find salvation through the younger generation. To justify his view he portrays Satyajit's character. Satyajit is a Gandhian character acting as the founder of Gandhigram where life is founded on discipline and self-restraint, similar to that of Gandhi's Sevagram. He controls the life of the village where Gandhian economics and ethics are worked out. With the supply of needs by the cottage-based industry besides food the village is self-sufficient. Land is owned by the Co-operative and food is distributed to each family according to its needs.

Every home has a spinning wheel. The basic scheme of craft centred teaching advocated by Gandhi is followed by the village in the sphere of education. The village sets new set of values—equality, fraternity and non-violence in thought and action. Gandhi's doctrine of celibacy or continence is advocated in the village. Satyajit himself adopts Brahmacharya after the birth of Sumita.

Non-violence, the major teaching of Gandhi, is propounded in the novel by Satyajit through his plan to form a Shanti Sena to Ladakh. He is a believer in the idea of dropping hatred for victory in the moral struggle.

Satyajit brings Suruchi and Sumita under the growing influence of his ideal known as Satyajitism. Satyajit has to resist against Bhashkar's aggression on Gandhigram. In spite of his failure in the former peace mission to Ladakh he wins a glorious success in the latter mission. This is really the victory of Satyajitism and non-violence.

In his village Satyajit continues the work of spiritual reconstruction by making the people renounce all. He dedicated his life to service and he uses the Gandhian instrument of "fast unto death" for protection of Gandhigram. By attaching little importance to material possession he cares for inner satisfaction. He discarded caste-system.

He is a man of stiff nature who would not move an inch even when the Government offers a compromise. So at last even the factory workers and even his opponent Bhashkar become one with him. The fast he undertakes is a challenge to the flesh, his vindication of the spirit's supremacy over the flesh. Thus he is the very soul of Gandhigram and the whole village follows his path. Another important character representing one of the two opposing points of view in debate is Bhashkar Roy, the Chief—Engineer of the Lohapur Steel Company. Since he is an American trained fellow his outlook is highly Westernised. He stands for three notions: steel standing for machines of mass production, steel representing the weapons for the country's defence and not to take vice as sin by avoiding all inhibitions. To him steel is the shaper of India's future. He keeps reverence for Satyajit. His steel temper is softened by his love for Sumita. The menace of China makes him vehement in his argument for industrialisation. He believes that only force can face the aggression.

Bhashkar is the exponent of the theory of industrialisation that should change the course of life and outlook and make life fuller and happier. He rebels against the conventional life full of inhibitions and against the arranged marriages in Indian society in which girls have to give themselves body and soul to the unknown men and live with them for all time. He favours the kind of love marriages of the machine age.

Bhashkar's love for Sumita heightens the romantic mood of the novel. Since he is a westernised engineer he wants an educated wife. He has the capacity to transform Sumita's life and outlook and win her hand. In spite of his long stay in America the Indianness in him cannot be obliterated. Rupa contrasts him with an English pilot who had made love to her in the past.

The character of Suruchi is important in the novel. She is the loyal partner of Satyajit both at home and in society. Her mind is dallying between her ideals and instincts; and her devotion to her husband and her interest in her daughter's life and prosperity. She surrenders her will to her husband and accepts his request to lead a life of Brahmacharya, though grudgingly. She cannot get over her longing for another child—a son. She admires the courage of the girl Jhanak. She pays due respect for her husband's friend Bireswar. At the end she triumphs over her husband who surrenders himself to her will. In the novel she moves first, from graceful naturalness to cramping asceticism and secondly, from inhibition to spontaneity and freedom. As a mother Suruchi knows the problems facing by her daughter Sumita and other girls. She also encourages Bhashkar's love for Sumita. She is against the idea of Sumita's leading a life of dedication. She blends in herself the qualities of asceticism and aestheticism to create a better society and happiness for herself and for all.

Sumita is a prominent woman character in the novel. She is tall, fair and shapely but unadorned. She is a girl grown and moulded according to the Gandhian pattern in a cocoon, with her father's ascetic ideal imprinted on her mind. She wears white but without kumkum mark and bangles. She is a playmate of Jhanak, the girl of the untouchables who is given to desires. Rupa and Jhanak are sharply contrasted to her. Her visit to Delhi widens her knowledge. It is this wider knowledge that enables her to work for a harmonious compromise between steeltown and Gandhigram. Finally, she comes out of the Satyajitism and blends in her the asceticism and the aestheticism, the spinning wheel and the turbine for making a better and happier society for herself and for all.

The character of Bireswar Basu deserves special mention in the novel. He plays a connecting link between Bhashkar and Suruchi. He is Satyajit's bosom friend always ready to help him in weal and woe.

The character of Mrs. Sorojini Mehra looms large in the development of the plot of the novel. She is the personal secretary of Bhashkar. She is the wife of a foreman at coke-oven battery. She is entrusted with confidential matters. She is vested with high responsibility. She can make a thorough welcome change in Bhashkar with her domineering quality. She faces women at the club. She conforms to the pervasive mother—image in Indian life. So she persuades Bhashkar, the C.E., to be the caretaker of the Chinese children. She has the courage to persuade even Rupa to leave when she senses a crisis due to her stay.

The character of Rupa is contrasted to that of Sumita. She is the daughter of an American mother and an Indian father. She is the stenographer in the office of Bhashkar. She was once an air hostess. While Sumita symbolises spinning wheel she symbolises the turbine. She takes care of the children of a Chinese prisoner Ah To. She is enamoured of the engineer Bhashkar. So she teaches the Chinese children in his house. She herself comes from a broken home and has a past. She is the sexy Anglo-Indian girl involved in romantic affairs with men.

The character of Jhanak is meant to be a contrast to the character of Sumita. There are other minor characters like Nandini and Ah To. They have significant roles in the novel. Ah To is introduced to be a bridge of understanding between China and India. Again, the character of Nandini's mother is but a sketch of the society ladies of Steeltown and of Delhi. "Number Two" is ambitious. She wants to top the list of women sacrificing for the motherland. The novelist institutes this character for skilful handling of comic irony. Thus the novel presents contrasts. Bhattacharya wants to show that in spite of the hostility between India and China, the hearts, at least of the younger generation, remain untouched by hatred.

Summing up: we can say that *Shadow from Ladakh* is a novel of great range and scope with a variety of characters. By telling a moving story the novel makes us feel the heart beats of a nation and presents the panorama of life on a vast canvas.

Regarding the style of the novel, there has been some improvement as compared to the style of his other novels. In this novel Bhattacharya's style achieves the Himalayan heights probably because he tackles a mighty theme. Certainly his style is mature and it moves with dignity as if to match with the heights of the action of the novel. Many political, scientific, military terms and slogans are being rung with the style of the novel. The slogan—"Hindi-Chini bhai bhai" still reverberates in our memory. In spite of the use of common devices like literal translation, metaphorical expressions, etc. Bhattacharya's style here becomes reflective and dignified.

6. *A Dream in Hawaii*: Bhattacharya's Prophecy about America

Bhabani Bhattacharya's sixth novel, perhaps the last of the novels so far written, *A Dream in Hawaii*, was written in America and published in 1978. It has for its subject the recurrence of the "Guru idea." Being the only novel written in America it has a locale more remote than that of his earlier novels and the issues are more diffused in it. It is Bhattacharya's attempt to catch the attention of America.

The novel maintains a dialective of ideas—bodily pleasure *Vs.* realisation of the ultimate Reality. Keeping this view in mind the novelist concludes the novel with the remark: "The Glimmer of the JAL aircraft faded into the night." "Glimmer" symbolises enlightenment which means realisation of the Ultimate Reality whereas "night" refers to "darkness" symbolising bodily pleasure. America not caring for poets but welcoming gurus like Bhattacharya himself, Yogis, gigolos, snake charmers and cooks of clandestine curries, forms the atmosphere of the thematic world of *A Dream in Hawaii.*

The theme of the novel relates to the clash of values represented by the East and the West; but it also incorporates and dilates upon the relationship between religion and art. Yogananda's view on the relationship of art and religion and Stella Gregson's musing on Swami Yogananda's religious quest have wide and strong implications in the context of the novel's multilayered theme. The novel, chronologically, covers the period beginning with the celebration of Swami Yogananda's hundred birthday in Hawaii after his leaving his ashram *Sadhna* in Rishikesh to accompany his American disciple Stella Gregson and his return trip to India after his dissociation from Dr. Vincent Swift's mercenary dream of a world yoga centre at Hawaii. Indeed, *A Dream in Hawaii* is Swami Yogananda's dream awakening the dormant Neeloy in himself. His return to his ashram is a journey of self-realisation.

Bhattacharya concentrates the story of the novel on three characters: Swami Yogananda, Dr. Vincent Swift and Devjani. In the American's way of life and its myriad aberrations such as the Transcendental Meditation, permissiveness, hippie culture, the use of tranquilisers, the Krishna consciousness and Hare Krishna, Hare Rama cult, Yogananda is an intruder but a disillusioned one.

Neeloy Mukherjee, metamorphosed into Swami Yogananda, was a Professor of Indian philosophy teaching in Indian universities for six years before he renounces the world. By the cumulative effect of his own spiritual hunger and the need and desire of his student paramour Devjani, he becomes a famed spiritual leader of India at thirty. In his travel in the U.S.A. he reaches Honolulu where he gives several lectures interpreting the Gita. He possesses wisdom and receives his mystical experience from Swami Vivekananda. Interpreting Vedanta as the path of self-knowledge filling the void between man and the infinite he also emphasises the need for physical exercises like breathing controlled with a precise set of techniques. He also explains his philosophy embodying "Sadhna."

But Neeloy is not wholly metamorphosed into Yogananda because he loves Devjani in an earthly sense. There is a world centre of Yogic Discipline coming up around Neeloy in Honolulu. This centre promises to provide the seekers of Hawaii, disenchanted with Western values, with Indian yoga as well as scope for research into the ancient occult lore. This project is the creation of Dr. Vincent Swift, a "Culture-Vulture."

In spite of Devjani's help to him in finding his new identity of a saint he remains thoroughly human throughout playing his role of a teacher and an ascetic. Finally, he is disillusioned and he discards his yellow garb. Leaving the vision of the World Centre dangling in the air and to the great dismay of Vincent Swift, he leaves for India. This escape is the only daring step he can decide upon in the prevailing circumstances.

The twenty chapters of the novel, falling into a neat thematic and structural pattern, depict the surfeit of sex as a symptom of the sick society in one half of them; while the other half exposes the true nature of spiritualism and salvation to be reached, according to the author, through self-fulfilment but not through self-denial.

Neeloy Mukherjee turned Yogananda and Devjani symbolise sexual sublimation. Jennifer, the young American socialite lady, seeking sexual satisfaction in the embrace of a New Delhi teen aged gigolo and of the shoeshine boys at the Sun Set Beach in Hawaii, represents sexual frustration. Stella Gregson's turning to the Indian Yogi to seek fulfilment of her spiritual needs by feeling revulsion for the kind of completely uninhibited four letter orgiastic sex demanded by her husband, Walt Gregson, shows sexual timidity. Dr. Vincent Swift, the president of Hawaii Akademi, who remains single after his wife's death, only to seek solace in furtively visiting x-rated films shows sexual inhibition.

Again, Devjani's mother, seeking solace in an adulterous relationship with the family doctor shows sexual frustration. Walt Gregson's quest for sexual thrills keeping longest with Sylvia Koo represents sexual aggressiveness or frustration. And then Frieda believing in the "Kamasutra" as the new gospel of America, after having a taste of "heavenly ambrosia" from an Indian charlatan guru, who thrills her with the display of tremendous sexual prowess, feels cheated when Yogananda refuses to oblige her with the gift of a similar seminal 'heavenly ambrosia.' Her act shows sexual aggressiveness.

Then the other side of the coin reveals the spiritual hunger of these sexual derelicts who follow the path shown by the Indian Yogi to understand the significance of "desireless" action and Vedantic concept of Ultimate Reality. Reaching the Ultimate Reality involves self-fulfilment instead of self-denial. Therefore, Yogananda has to return to India to wait for Devjani to accept him only as Neeloy.

Bhattacharya makes a successful portrayal of characters in the novel. The chief character is Yogananda. He is young, tall and clean-shaven. He is a man of mystery from the East. He is ageless and rootless. His relentless quest is directed to the core of reality behind the illusory appearances. He is taken as a Neo-Buddha to lead Americans from darkness to light. He follows the traditional ways of inner purification by lecturing on the topic "Crisis in a sick society." He is a world citizen in whom the East and the West easily coalesced.

The character of Devjani plays a significant part in the novel. It is she who has put Neeloy on the mystic path. Again, it is his passion for her which proves to be the greatest hurdle in his progress on the mystic path. This passion itself in a way saves him from the beak of the culture-vulture. Later, she has been granted a research fellowship by the East-West Centre in Honolulu. She is the daughter of the famed nuclear scientist at Calcutta's Shah Institute. She is caught in her intense need for change. She watches the visage of Varanasi with its multiple splendour—a fusion in which the spiritual and the intellectual become united and inseparable.

Bhattacharya also delineates other characters significantly. Characters like Vincent Swift, Walt Gregson and Sylvia Koo, all pouncing upon Yogananda with their various motives, may very well symbolise the hostile forces which stalk a half baked Yogi to make him their easy prey at the opportune time. Dr. Vincent Swift is portrayed as the prototype of the twentieth century culture-vulture. Jennifer is depicted as a young socialite seeking spiritual help after her years of unfulfilled sexual relationship with her husband. Professor Walt Gregson, a votary of sexual permissiveness, is a man who uses his mistress, Sylvia Koo, as a weapon to breach the Yogi's seeming detachment.

Other minor characters like Sylvia Koo, Stella Gregson, Frieda, etc. are also fascinatingly delineated but finally they have faded into insignificance. Frieda is delineated as a woman believing in the *Kamasutra*.

One of the concerns of the novel is that money monopolisers are far from being spiritual. Again, mystics with meagre spiritual power fall easy victims to those money monopolisers. The novel reflects American life in its true colours. The new permissive age free from inhibitions and taboos, is shown vividly. And it is suggested that every nine minutes there will be at least one reported case of rape.

The novel shows Americans as crazy about stars. They exchange Technology for Astrology. In the American society men and women should be equally free to achieve their sexual self-discovery. Taking tranquilisers, to be rid of tension and to forget wretchedness, is their habit.

Bhattacharya also exposes the Extrasensory perception which is quite common in India. He depicts the core of Indian faith in spiritualism involving actions which are free from desire for their fruits. Referring to the magnetic influence of four personalities—Gautama Buddha, Vivekananda, Tagore and Gandhi, Bhattacharya depicts the Indian spiritual scene. Bhattacharya shows his disillusionment at the callous indifference of the Indians towards Gandhi and his ideals. Moreover, Bhattacharya refers to the two forces—the gospel of Hare Krishna Movement and the concept of Transcendental Meditation that have swayed the lives of the people the world over.

Kamasutra, the ancient classic of India dealing with the ways lovers have to kiss, their love-play and techniques for the partner's arousal to the right pitch with 30 illustrative ways of sexual act is also referred to in the novel. Bhattacharya satirises spiritual charlatanism and presents a critique of the bourgeois value system making profitable business venture even out of yoga.

All characters discover that the nauseating stink of the "dead rat...under the nylon rug" cannot be removed by cosmetic cleansing. There is a suggestion that the dead rat, which is nothing but the decadent capitalism, should be thrown out in the vital interest of the common mass. This is where, of course, Bhattacharya is unforgivably hysterical. He desperately tries to say something new about America and takes refuge in histrionics. Bhattacharya makes occasional descriptions of natural beauty in

Hawaii islands. He also portrays characters to suit the situation and atmosphere in which his plot is developed. The novelist's aim in the novel may be good but the presentation does not hit the mark of his earlier novels discussed in the first part of this chapter. He is hardly free himself from the rotten cliches and gimmicking that characterise Indian spiritual charlatanism.

But Bhattacharya's technique employed in this novel serves his purpose well. He uses the technique of Conradian shifts in time—mingling and fracturing past, present and future to develop the psychic and spiritual make up of his human characters. The theme easily lends itself to the creation of stereotype characters. All characters remain rooted to the earth in the midst of an ambience saturated with a supercilious craze for everything "super," ranging from super-technology to super-sadhana of super-stars in a super-civilisation. He also makes judicious use of flashback and montage technique so often used in cinematography to capture truth. Picking up the protagonist at a specific point in time the reader is provided with the information about the earlier phase of his life through intermittent flashbacks. It also reveals the past of the characters coming in close contact with him.

Bhattacharya makes the opening scene of this novel very significant from the narrative point of view. The novel opens with Swami Yogananda talking to his image in the mirror, musing on his age and closes with his conversation on the phone with Hawaii Academy's president Dr. Vincent Swift, about the celebration of his hundredth birthday. Within this short span are exposed almost all important characters and the various thematic issues of the novel.

From the above analysis it is found that Bhattacharya is a man of interculturation. The East-West Centre helps in growing up this interculturation. The University of Hawaii with its motto; "Above all nations is humanity" influences in expanding his inter-cultural ideas. Bhattacharya is a multicultural person meditating between several groups in a culturally diverse world.

He is a meditating man bridging the East and West and concerning with the synthesis of old and new. All this is good and great and we admire Bhattacharya's art of self-glorification and moral posturing but how all this helps the novel is not clear.

In *A Dream in Hawaii* Bhattacharya's style is plain, devoid of similes and metaphors of earlier works, devoid of the dignified and elevated style that had characterised *Shadow from Lakakh.* Again the references to pubic hair, the different sizes of the navels, the four-letter word used for sex art and other vulgar expressions mar the beauty of the novel. They also reveal the meanest level to which Bhattacharya has degraded himself as a writer in order to jump into the bandwagon, as if all that would Americanise his style in a fortuitous use of four-letter word. *A Dream in Hawaii* is the sensation day-dream of a self-deceived Messiah.

REFERENCES

1. G.P. Sarma: *Nationalism in Indo-Anglian Fiction* (New Delhi: Sterling Publishers, 1978), 227.
2. Bhabani Bhattacharya : *So Many Hungers*! (Delhi: Orient Paperbacks, 1978), 93. All subsequent quotations are from this edition.
3. Bhattacharya 25.
4. K.R. Chandrasekharan: *Bhabani Bhattacharya* (New Delhi: Arnold Heinemann, 1974), 11.
5. Chandrasekharan 11.
6. Chandrasekharan 34.
7. Bhabani Bhattacharya, *Music for Mohini* (Delhi: Orient Paperbacks, 1952), 67. All subsequent quotations are from this edition.
8. *Music for Mohini* 67.
9. *Music for Mohini* 94.
10. B. Shyamala Rao, *Bhabani Bhattacharya & His Works* (Bareilly: Students Store, n.d.), 44.
11. Chandrasekharan 56.
12. Shyam M. Asnani, *Critical Response to Indian Anglish Fiction* (Delhi: Mittal Publications, 1985), 7.
13. Chandrasekharan 56.

14. Chandrasekharan 58.
15. Bhabani Bhattacharya, *He Who Rides a Tiger* (Delhi: Hindpocket Books, 1955), 39. All subsequent quotations are from this edition.
16. Chandrasekharan 63.
17. *He Who Rides a Tiger,* 232.
18. *He Who Rides a Tiger,* 54.
19. Sarma 268.

4

Theme of Earlier Novels and Critical Outlook

During the period of more than 30 years from 1947 to 1978, Bhabani Bhattacharya experienced life in two different worlds—the Spiritualist East and the Materialist West. So novels written in India have different themes from that of the novel written during his stay in America. The first five novels which were written in India: *So Many Hungers!*, *Music for Mohini, He Who Rides a Tiger, A Goddess Named Gold and Shadow from Ladakh* may be treated as earlier novels dealing with the common themes as discussed in Chapter 3 whereas the sixth novel—*A Dream in Hawaii,* written in America, deals with the bourgeois values system, sex, yoga, the Guru theme, mysticism and materialism.

Regarding the theme of his earlier novels R.K. Badal remarks:

> "In his earlier novels Dr. Bhattacharya depicts the horrors of war and famine, pestilence, clash of traditions, ignorance, misguided faith in religion, superstitions, casteism, economic and food crisis."[1]

These themes are finely presented with a skilful handling of technique and in these novels the novelist tries to propound his theory of literature and view on social and moral function of art which are briefly discussed below. These discussions are made from his own articles and statements to interviewers. Although he has his own definite views on art and fiction, he has not compiled them in a book form like E.M. Forster. Bhattacharya can hardly be ranked with Forster as a critic having neither professional skill nor any worthwhile insight into what makes literary works *literary*. On the whole, he is amateurish and platitudinous.

The first thing in his theory of literature and art is his pleading for reality in literature. He focuses his attention on the creative artist's concern with social or historical reality. According to him, a true work of art can be created only when an artist is able to achieve the fusion of the reality of the old times with that of his own age (whatever that means). He observes:

> "A work of art, —romantic or classical, old or new, must convey truth, the truth of emotion, which is the ultimate realism."[2]

He also emphasises the importance of the personal experiences of life of the artist who should carefully look around him to grasp the world of the people he happens to live with in order to make his picture realistic. And supporting this view Bhattacharya himself remarks:

> "Unless a writer has a keen observation and an eye for noting the details of general behaviour of folks, he cannot write a social novel. I have developed this habit and I have not missed a single opportunity of observing incidents, happenings, where I can gain something for the writer in me."[3]

Rejecting the dictum of "Art for Art's Sake" Bhattacharya upholds the concept of "Art for Life's Sake." In his view, a novel should be concerned with social reality. Emphasising the purposiveness of art and the social purpose of a novel he holds the following remark:

> "...I hold that a novel must have a social purpose. It must place before the reader something from the society's point of view. Art is not necessarily for art's sake. Purposeless art and literature which is much in vogue does not appear to me a sound judgment."[4]

Professor K.K. Sharma is right in interpreting Bhattacharya's view on the creative artist's having a deep-root in human life in the following words:

> "Though fascinated and inspired by nature and its manifestations, the artist is deeply rooted in human life, and it is especially true of the novelist and the dramatist."[5]

Bhattacharya himself holds the view that it is the dramatist and the novelist who give him his creative fire, and not nature because:

> "...the novel and the drama, the two forms of creative art that have almost replaced the epic and the lyric, are wholly concerned with the human scene."[6]

Bhattacharya is of the view that art is inalienable from truth and invariably presents it, though not dogmatically but dramatically and emotionally, in terms of life.

Emphasising the artist's inevitable concern with truth and reality Bhattacharya observes:

> "...the creative writer's final business is to reveal the truth. He reveals it, unlike the philosopher, in no cold statements of dogma but only in terms of life, rendered through the devices of dramatisation. How could the truth help being partisan?"[7]

In fact, the depiction of truth, as an artist sees it, leads him to keep the ethical values in his art. So he should fearlessly depict the truth as he sees it but not to interfere with the pure spirit of his creative art because it should reveal the basic truth of life artistically. Conforming to this fact Bhattacharya holds his view on the moral value of art. Regarding the artist's preaching of morals in his art Bhattacharya remarks:

> "Art must preach, but unobtrusively, by its vivid interpretation of life. Art must preach, but only by virtue of its being a vehicle of truth. If that is propaganda, there is no need to eschew the word."[8]

Bhattacharya is against the view of critics like C. Paul Verghese who says:

> "An artist who turns recent event into fiction, cannot easily succeed; for the unconscious mind requires much time to perform its wonder of transmuting incident into art."[9]

Rejecting such argument he is of the view that a creative artist possesses a well-developed sensitivity by means of which everything he happens to see or experience is to impress and haunt him more than what he feels and knows indirectly through books. Citing the example of Tolstoy's *War and Peace* where the novelist's descriptions of war are based on the war that actually took place in which he himself was a soldier fighting to save Sevastopol, Bhattacharya opines that even the historical novelist depends more on personal experiences than on the knowledge and information acquired through books and imagination.

Bhattacharya really opposes the view of the critics that a piece of writing concerning contemporary events may degenerate into more journalism. According to him, even contemporary events can form a suitable theme for a novel. In defence of this view he differentiates journalistic literature from a genuine work of art by saying that the former does not emanate from inner urges and does not have spontaneity, while the latter should have both these elements. Distinguishing the two types of writing Bhattacharya observes:

> "A novelist may well be concerned with today, the current hour or moment, if it is meaningful for him, if it moves him sufficiently into emotional response. An instance that comes to my mind among a score of others is Steinbeck's *The Grapes of Wrath*. That good book, depicting an immediate and acute problem of the time of its writing, could easily have become brilliant journalism. Instead, it became a true piece of fiction."[10]

Bhattacharya holds the view that sex can be a suitable theme for artistic expression. Since sex constitutes an integral part of human life, it is bound to have an important expression in literature. It becomes beautiful and not repulsive when a good work of art treats it meaningfully and suggestively. Extolling D.H. Lawrence and Ernest Hemingway for their artistic and meaningful treatment of sex in their writings by making it a dignified subject matter for great literature Bhattacharya remarks:

> "The flow of cheap, paperbacked, vulgar, low-taste books revelling in sex-descriptions cannot be welcome. I have a revulsion for them. But look at Lawrence. He creates a whole world of this much tabooed-feeling and yet the descriptions are most beautiful and excel in their lyrical quality. Look at Hemingway and you will learn how sex can be a theme to write upon, without making it repulsive."[11]

But Bhattacharya is all for moderation and restraint in the treatment of love and depiction of sex inartistically by the "so-called romantic writer."

According to Bhattacharya a novelist may or may not have a pre-conceived plot. When he strikes upon a theme and ready to write upon it, he may or may not think of the beginning, middle and end of his novel. His duty is to invent characters and events and then to start writing that never ends the way he planned at the start. The entire original fabric of the book is changed because characters and situations govern his narrative. About this particular method of his writing he remarks:

> "When I feel like writing upon a theme, and the characters and events fit in the pattern, I start putting it down on paper. But once I start writing, it is not I, but the characters and situations that compel me to be led by them. It is they who decide the way they should end.... The end of the story, in my case, is never the one which I had in my mind in the beginning. Even the original plan itself gets modified or changed due to certain traits which my characters develop during the course of events. It will be therefore a violence if I stick to my original plan while the characters change."[12]

It is an important observation of Bhattacharya that a novel should not be the result of writing for the sake of writing. Since it is not carefully planned it ought to be spontaneous and should proceed from the writer's inner compulsions. To affirm this view he aptly states:

> "I have not believed in writing for the sake of writing. I seldom planned a story structure. Each story grew in my subconscious mind, as it were. When it had grown enough, I had to give it physical form. The characters, even when I had decided how they were going to behave, moved by their own volition, often defeating my purpose."[13]

Bhattacharya sticks to his own theory of fiction that contemporary events and social realities are suitable subjects for writing novels. So he deals with contemporary Indian problems in all his novels. Actually the Bengal Famine of 1943 and the Quit India Movement of 1942 inspired him to write—*So Many Hungers*! and *He Who Rides a Tiger*. The synthesis of old and new values in Indian life urged him to write *Music for Mohini*. *A Goddess Named Gold* is concerned with the meaning and significance of freedom while *Shadow from Ladakh* focuses attention on problems arising out of the Indo-China border conflict in 1962. Had he not chosen such contemporary problems for his themes he would not have become a novelist. Answering the question how he became a novelist he writes:

> "When I was a student in London in the thirties, I started writing novel. Halfway through, I thought it was no good and I was not destined to be a creative writer. I tore up the manuscript. However, I wrote some short sketches for *The Spectator*. I translated Tagore. Back in India I found other preoccupations. Early in the forties, I tried to do a novel again. When half written, it found its way into a heap of unwanted papers.
>
> Then the great Bengal Famine swept down upon Bengal. The emotional stirrings I felt (more than two million men, women and children died of slow starvation

> amid a man-made scarcity) were a sheer compulsion to creativity. The result was the novel *So Many Hungers*!"[14]

Indeed, Bhattacharya was deeply influenced by Tagore and John Steinbeck. He derived some of the philosophical ideas introduced in *Music for Mohini* and *Shadow from Ladakh* from Tagore. His translation of Tagore's works—*The Golden Boat* and his writing of *Towards Universal Man* show that he admired the great poet.

Bhattacharya has a definite theory of the novel which he applies to his own works. It is essential to examine and analyse further the themes of his earlier novels in order to know how he correlated and applied his theory of fiction to them.

Bhattacharya's first novel *So Many Hungers*! as we have seen in Chapter 3, deals with the contemporary Indian social problems. One aspect of the problems explored in the novels is its realistic depiction of the miserable village life of the contemporary India.

In his visit to the village Rahoul meets Devata (Dadu) with whom he discusses the village life of Baruni which represents the life in Indian villages. In the course of their conversation Dadu tells Rahoul about the miserable plight of the landless *Kisans* of Baruni village in the following words:

> "Facts never tell much unless they are seen in terms of human experience. On his petty income the landed peasant can have just enough of his own rice to eat, no reserve for lean days. And the Kisans—they must always be hungry, save for a spell of two or three months in the year, when they earn meals and a wage for field-work. The hundred million Kisans of India must always be hungry. It is a rare gracious day to have the stomach full."[15]

Another remarkable aspect is the book's depiction of the city life. Through the conversation of Rahoul and his wife Monju we know much about the ways of young men and women in the city. They tease one another. The boys wink at girls. The girls enjoy a lot of freedom. They dance publicly and wear fashionable dresses, leaving their arms, shoulders, backs and parts of breast bare. The notions of social status and snobbery create gulf of difference between man and man. Rahoul remarks that only high Government officials are thought to be important. So one tries to occupy a high position in the Government offices. Distinction between the high and the low, the rich and the poor is vividly depicted in the book.

The Second novel *Music for Mohini*, reflects post-independence social changes the details of which have been discussed in Chapter 3. By portraying the hero Jayadev as a character in whom the time-honoured Indian traditions fuse with the elements of modernisation the novelist aims at bringing a social renaissance, attainment of full stature by man in the society.

The novel also cites reference to caste-system prevailing in the contemporary Indian social life. The Brahmin boy Heeralal does not touch meat under the impact of his grandmother. The novel also pictures the problem of marriage faced by the parents. Mohini's marriage shows how parents are restless and busy to find a suitable bridegroom. Mohini's father advertised her in the matrimonial column of the daily newspapers. There is also reference to the act of bride showing. Dowry is a factor that will at times decide the problem of marriages.

Moreover, this novel refers to the superstitions and rituals prevailing in the then society. Heeralal's wearing of an amulet, Mohini's paying respect to a white owl, Mohini's offering of blood to the virgin Goddess (*Devi*) for begetting a son are instances of people's blind belief in ritual. Besides, the importance of horoscope and astrology is also referred to in the novel in the act of Professor Hanuman's advertisement for reading man's life correctly.

The practice of restraining food to Mohini on her marriage day and the old Mother's helplessness in not seeing Mohini off with her husband to the railway station are instances of blind rituals prevailed in the then society. The old practice of elders giving advice to the bride is also mentioned realistically in the book. Besides these, numerous other rituals, customs and ceremonies are hinted in the novel. The act of Mohini's showing her saries and marriage jewels to her husband's people is a way of observing a time-honoured convention.

Social reformations by abolishing the customs of child marriage and ban on the widow re-marriage are vividly depicted in the novel through the intention of Jayadev. The novel also criticises the caste-system.

Bhattacharya's third novel *He Who Rides a Tiger*, reflects the degrading political and economic system in the caste-ridden society of the early forties. The central character Kalo and his daughter Chandralekha are portrayed as sufferers from the degraded economy and caste-system. But Kalo revenges against the caste-Hindus and the rich by becoming the priest of a fake Shiva statue. By championing the downtrodden he becomes "a legend of freedom."

The book also depicts the unbridgeable gulf between the rich and the poor; the high and the low. Kalo pities the poor people dying slowly from the hunger created by the rich for their profit. There is also reference to the problem of marriage of a boy and a girl of the same caste. Kalo is unable to find a suitable match for his daughter's marriage in his own caste. Even when his daughter wins a medal for her merit she does not get a due applause due to her low-caste parentage. This shocks Kalo and he remarks:

> "Imagine if the magistrate's daughter had won the medal how the town would have rejoiced and feted her!"[16]

As discussed in Chapter 3, the novel criticises the caste system in the society. Kalo feels hatred of the caste system when he hears the tragic story of his jailmate Biten's sister Purnima due to caste-system. The evil effects of caste-system make Biten discard Brahminism in his future life.

But Kalo wants to wreak vengeance against this social evil. On the advice of Biten he pretends to be a Brahmin priest of a fake Shiva temple although he is a low-born Kamar. Disguising as Mangal Adhikari, he befools the rich and the high caste-people. Thus he breaks the age-old social custom.

Kalo sees three social cruelties torturing the life of the poor and the low-caste people through his own experience. They are—innocent poor girls going to harlot house under compulsion, innocent poor persons' imprisonment for minor lapses and the animal like life of the prisoners in the prison. He himself finds his daughter in the brothel. He thinks that she will be condemned as fallen woman. Again, he himself has been imprisoned for stealing a mere banana and once again he suffers much in the jail where he works like an oxen. So Kalo and Biten successfully hit back the rich and the high caste Hindus. Thus Bhattacharya's attack on the repulsive realities of Indian social life is vividly reflected in the novel.

Bhattacharya's fourth novel *A Goddess Named Gold*, gives a vivid account of the Indian village life and society of the time of Independence. As we have seen in Chapter 3 one remarkable social picture in the book is woman's suffering from the acute shortage of cloths caused by the profiteer, the Seth of Sonamitti, the only cloth merchant in the region, for his profit. The village women, led by the Seth's wife Lakshmi, launch a movement against him and get saries.

The novel vividly depicts the election method practically conducted by the politicians of the time through the activities of the Seth. He hires propagandists to convince the people that he is a brother and equal of the poor. He plans for sending squads of young teachers from the village school to shout slogans in his favour up and down the village streets.

Once again the caste-evil and superstitions eating out the Indian village society are clearly depicted in this novel. The caste difference and its bad effect is seen in the case of the village middle-aged Halwai who wants to marry young Meera, a girl of different caste. The villagers are as much oppressed by superstitions as the casteism. The villagers' belief in the miraculous power of Meera's amulet given by her grandfather, is due to their superstitious idea. As mentioned in Chapter 3 there is also reference to the villagers' belief in the horoscope and the improbable legend of the talking goat.

The novel also reflects the evil effects of dowry and bribery in Indian society. Parents are shown to be quite broken down due to shortage of money for the dowry of their bridal daughters.

Besides these things, the novel realistically depicts the system of bribery and corruption prevailing in the then society. There are references to the dishonest contractors' building substandard bridges and buildings but not punished by the corrupt government. Thus the novel, reflecting the various social realities of the time, correlates Bhattacharya's theory of fiction.

The fifth novel *Shadow from Ladakh* depicts many social realities of the post-Independence India. The need for overlooking caste-system for the betterment of the society is emphasised in this novel. Satyajit, who is a devotee of Tagore in Santiniketan, rejects his surname 'Sen' to become casteless and rootless like Yogis. He marries Suruchi, a girl from a different caste without any hesitation. They run a happy family by eradicating caste distinctions. Gandhigram is also depicted as aiming to eradicate casteism and untouchability. All men in this village are equal in status since they are all casteless.

The novel also refers to the population explosion which is becoming a problem to the national life of India. Bhashkar is portrayed to be afraid of this horrible problem of the birth of a child for every five seconds in India. And the idea of feeding, rearing, clothing, educating, giving cultural welfare, giving employment and giving their due shares of human existence of these babies harasses Bhashkar.

Finally, the novel vividly pictures the political condition of India, China and Tibet around the year 1962. It also reflects well and effectively portrays war scenes invested with abundance of human interest.

Thus Bhattacharya's own theory of fictional art is tactfully applied and correlated in this novel by depicting the truth and contemporary realities. In this regard we can quote Prof. K.K. Sharma's significant remark:

> *Shadow from Ladakh* thoroughly examines the various planes of reality—political, historical, social, economic, moral and spiritual.[17]

REFERENCES

1. R.K. Badal, *Indo-Anglian Literature: An Outline* (Bareilly: Prakash Book Depot, 1975), 53.
2. *Literature and Social Reality,* The Aryan Path, Vol. XXVI, No. 9 (Sept. 1955), 392.
3. Sudhakar Joshi, "An Evening with Bhabani," *The Sunday Standard,* (April 27, 1969), VII.
4. Sudhakar Joshi VII.
5. K.K. Sharma, *Bhabani Bhattacharva: His Vision and Themes* (New Delhi: Abhinav Publications, 1979), 121.
6. *Literature and Social Reality* 394.
7. *Literature and Social Reality* 394.
8. *Literature and Social Reality* 394.
9. C. Paul Verghese, "The Problems of Indian Novelist in English," *The Banasthali Patrika,* No. 12 (Jan. 1969).
10. Iqbal Bakhtiyar (ed.), *The Novel in Modern India* (Bombay: P.E.N. Centre, 1964), 47.
11. Sudhakar Joshi VII.
12. Sudhakar Joshi VII.
13. *Contemporary Novelists in the English Language* (New York: St. Martin's Press, 1972), 38, quoted in K.R. Chandrasekharan's *Bhabani Bhattacharya* (New Delhi: Arnold-Heinemann, 1974), 2.
14. Chandrasekharan 2.
15. Bhabani Bhattacharya, *So Many Hunqers*! (Bombay: Jaico Publishing House, 1964), 22.
16. Bhabani Bhattacharva, *He Who Rides a Tiger* (Delhi: An Orient Paperback, Hind Pocket Books (P) Ltd., 1955), 143.
17. Sharma, 146.

5

Another Perspective on Bhattacharya's Art (His Affirmative Vision)

Like Mulk Raj Anand, the writer with leftist leanings but unlike R.K. Narayan and Raja Rao both of whom have some philosophical depth, Bhabani Bhattacharya, a compeer to the above trio, has explored and depicted an affirmative vision of life in all his novels. Emphasising the affirmation of life in Bhattacharya's novels Dr. K.K. Sharma remarks:

> "Even in the midst of ghastly and heart-rending scenes of human sufferings and tortures, life asserts itself sparkling amid ashes. From this assertion of ethical values and the synthesis of the old and the new and of opposite extremes emanates Bhabani Bhattacharya's final vision of the affirmation of life."[1]

Let us look again at the novels, starting with *So Many Hungers!* Bhattacharya's affirmative view is seen even in the opening of the novel. In fact, Chapter 1 of the book opens with two exciting things—the evil effects of World War II and the labour pangs of Monju and concludes with Rahoul's sense of fulfilment, and elation and faith in a new world order which are described by the novelist as:

> "The elation has made his heart swell! Two exciting things had happened to him this autumn day. The Prime Minister of Britain had declared war on the Swastika. Monju had given birth to a baby girl. Either event was a profound experience that made his emotions vibrate, as though he had achieved some personal fulfilment. In

> the blood bath of war much else would be frowned besides the Swastika. A million youths would not die in vain."[2]

Chapter 2 opens with Rahoul's high hopes on a bright new day. Monju has become a mother with her baby as the image of joy and the Allied Powers have declared war against the Swastika. And these two things give him the idea of fullness of life, an affirmation, and not a negation of life. Again, Rahoul is hopeful about the aftermath of the horrible global war because he is convinced that suffering purifies human souls. Prophesying this purification he aptly remarks:

> "In the agonies of war, the soul of humankind would be cleansed.
>
> Humankind after the war would not be the humankind of before."[3]

Rahoul believes in the theory of goodness of people everywhere. In spite of his own father's being merciless profiteer, he tries to help poor people. He even brings pregnant women to his house and helps them. Thus the presence of the true life-spirit throbbing with happiness seen in him by his wife is expressed thus:

> "...her husband's true spirit, his hunger for a happier life for the common man."[4]

Bhattacharya's faith in the greatness of life is depicted through Devta, who is called *Dadu* by Rahoul. Rahoul believes in Devta's power of inciting him with faith in life and so he goes to him even after he acquires the highest academic qualification. The novelist's high opinion of the goodness of the country people is expressed through Devta's words:

> "...Centuries of hardship and strain have not destroyed their faith in human values."[5]

Devta is indeed an embodiment of ideal life characterised by dignity, courage, grandeur and strength. Whoever comes in contact with him is infused with hope and strength. Whenever gloomy and idle, Rahoul goes to him to get hope and inspiration because:

> "...*Dadu* would strengthen his spirit, *Dadu* had strengthened him even in the past with his clear faith and vision."[6]

Bhattacharya portrays Kajoli also as an incarnation of affirmation, nobility and fullness of life. She has trust in the worthiness and greatness of life since she inherits the traditional values and manners of India, unaffected and undefiled by modern attitudes and notions. The novelist describes her quality through Devta's words spoken to Rahoul:

> "She has a legacy of manners as old as India. How could she give up her manners and proprieties to suit your new fangled city ideas."[7]

Bhattacharya's view on life's nobility through noble and idealistic acts of man is depicted through Rahoul's younger brother Kunal's going to war by resisting even the strongest pressure of his mother. He resigns his post for another man's chance to get it, and remarks that he does not fear to live dangerously and participates the World War II.

Bhattacharya shows his men and women as heroic, courageous and true fighters inspired by the vision of a just social order. We see such quality in the members of Kajoli's family. Speaking of the novelist's portrayal of such character Dr. Harish Raizada significantly remarks:

> "Bhattacharya portrays full-blooded men and women, creatures of their society, victims of its unjust persecutions and yet possessing invincible strength to carry the manner of high ideals of new India."[8]

Even after the arrest of her father and her young brother Kanu, Kajoli and Onu work in the field gleefully and vigorously in the scorching sun. They are not weakened by oppression and terror but rather they are strengthened. Through their acts the novelist depicts the villagers as the embodiment of robust life, full of energy and fearlessness. Hard work does not subdue Kajoli's faith in Dadu's ideal—"Be Strong. Be true. Be deathless."

One instance of affirmation of life is seen through small boy Onu's dauntless striving to face life. He has to live on roots, herbs and figs as other poor children do. He collects figs even at the risk of falling down from the top of the tree. He is determined to collect enough to save his mother and sister, and the little brothers and sisters of his friend. Although he does not escape from the adverse circumstances of life, still he is kind, courageous and hopeful. This is shown by the remark:

> "Everyday we'll go halves, bhai, halves. That tree has plenty left."
>
> "…Every little branch at the top I can reach with my hand."[9]

Bhattacharya shows famished people as possessing high ideals and sacrificial spirit through Kajoli's mother who cannot bear the sight of a desperate, starving young woman with no milk in her breasts for her dying baby. She gives her their cow Mangala and also tries to lead her to the bright and gay life in Calcutta and says:

> "Why girl, you can go to Calcutta City; you never thought of that!" …You will find work, big wages! Nothing to worry about—nothing."[10]

The novelist depicts an affirmative vision of life through the journey of Kajoli, her mother and brother Onu to Calcutta for earning their livelihood. On the way they see famished people more worn than them. Inspired by this sight these three persons come out triumphantly in their ordeal and this vividly projects the novelist's attitude of affirmation towards life which is described thus:

> "New wicks of strength burned in her. In desperate crisis she had made herself strong for her children. And her children, too, were strong for Mother and for each other. Weakness in one would have destroyed all."[11]

Bright and positive values of life like repentence, sacrifice, kindness, dignity, self-respect, gratitude, hard labour, etc. are also referred to through a kind soldier's saving Kajoli's life with the aid of a military doctor. Seeing his kindness and sacrifice Kajoli's mother expresses her gratitude.

> "'Live long, my son'.... 'Live long'...God's blessing upon all of you who are kind."[12]

The novelist's affirmative vision of life is reflected through the heroic and sacrificial act of a destitute maid. This maid earns money by showing her breasts to men for feeding the famished people who call her "the Mother" and to whom she is life and joy. The same supreme sacrifice is seen in the act of a destitute old man's surrendering his free food card to Rahoul for the sake and use of a more needy person.

Bhattacharya also projects his affirmative vision of life in Samarendra Basu. When his younger son Kunal, who is in the military service, is declared missing, though deeply shocked, he does not give up hope. Moreover, he is proud of the heroism of his son, Rahoul, when he is arrested by the British Government. The novelist also carries an affirmative attitude towards war by remarking that it is desirable if it is used as a means of freeing the world from pests. Again, the suicide of an old man proving himself undefeated in the face of the famine is the projection of the author's affirmation of life.

Bhattacharya portrays Rahoul as a courageous, heroic, dignified and patriotic fellow. When he is arrested he is free from the fear of suffering and loneliness. He worries only for the people. Similarly, Rahoul's wife, Monju is not shocked when she comes to know of Rahoul's arrest, rather she is calm, strong with some hidden strength, and she declares her desire to follow his path.

The novelist's firm belief in the affirmative aspect of life is reflected in the last scene where Rahoul is reaching the prison thronged with famished people beaming with exultation. This exultation is described as:

> "There was no defeat in the voices, but a secret, excited triumph.... Listening, Rahoul began to lose his sadness, for in that instant he saw past the clouds of pain—he saw the horizon of the east illumined by a new dawn.... And a strong exultation burned in his eyes and a strange instance look of conquest kindled in his face as he gave his voice to the united voices:
>
> 'The more they tighten the chains
> The more the chains loosen!'"[13]

Such analysis of the major scenes and episodes of the novel shows Bhattacharya's conviction in the affirmation of life. We agree with Dr. K.K. Sharma who remarks:

> "The novel is, indeed...an artistic embodiment of his affirmative vision of life."[14]

Bhattacharya's second novel *Music for Mohini* also carries his view on the affirmative aspect of life. The central character, Mohini, is portrayed as having a passion for the bright, joyful life and a contempt for all that is dull and dead. She resolves to adjust herself with the new environment in the Big House. Speaking of her decision the novelist states:

> "But she had her husband. For his sake she would absorb new ways of thought and habit, cultivate new interests."[15]

Making a synthesis of opposites Bhattacharya presents positive aspect of life. The city-bred modern girl Mohini is made to live in harmony with her orthodox and traditional mother-in-law. Again, there arises a harmonious adjustment and solution of the conflict between Jayadev's mother and her opponents: Jayadev, Mohini and others. A synthesis appears when the opposite forces understand each other. And bridging the gap between the old and the new Bhattacharya remarks:

> "...and for the first time, she could see her son clearly,.... In that moment of insight, the mother almost understood her son and, through him, the new revolt, the restless spirit of the new dawn."[16]

Bhattacharya portrays Mohini finding fullness and fulfilment in life by doing simple act of educating illiterate village women. Explaining her position and fulfilment in the new life Bhattacharya remarks:

> "Life in Behula had been hard at first, even drab and tiresome, but she had conquered the strain and had built a life for herself with a great brightness, a life of fulfilment."[17]

The novelist expresses his idea of opposing denial of life by pleading for people's recognition of Sudha. He makes the rational forces, led by Harindra and Jayadev, win over the traditional superstitious forces led by the village priest and thereby reflects his affirmative view of life. Towards the end of the novel Jayadev enjoys a happy life with his wife Mohini by bridging the gulf between themselves. The novelist significantly describes Mohini's happy and harmonious life thus:

> "At last, there was no discord. Life was music—a note of song for the old Mother was in her, a note for Jayadev and his rebel gods, a note for the Big House and Behula village, torn and at cross purposes for a while. Her life was music—the true quest for every woman, her deepest need."[18]

Bhattacharya's third novel *He Who Rides a Tiger* also reflects his positive view of life through its central character Kalo, a poor village blacksmith. The novelist also expresses his firm belief and positive attitude to life by showing the lofty ideals of the poor villagers. As an instance, starving people like Kalo spits on the faces of procurers of Calcutta brothels. Even in the most desperate state of hunger, they keep their high ideals and they do not commit suicide as they have a firm belief in the preservation of life, rather than in its destruction.

The novelist shows the helpless people's courage and belief in the positive aspects of life through Kalo and his daughter. They can compensate for their past loss not by losing their heart at any tragic situation. Even when Motichand proposes to marry

Lekha, she does not lose heart. Instead of contemplating suicide, she sees life before her and the situation is described by the novelist as:

> "Life stood before her—not death. There was a new strength in her, a new awareness, with which to face the challenge of an unknown future."[19]

Bhattacharya's conviction in a positive, bright view of life is expressed through the life history of Kalo who dupes the high-caste people and upsets the social order by investing himself with Brahminhood and coming on the top of the society. Describing his triumph over society Bhattacharya metaphorically remarks:

> "They had come back in time to hear him, to see him drive his steel deep into the tiger. The scum of the earth had hit back, hit back where it hurt."[20]

Kalo's brave confession is cheered by the common folks and by this time Lekha is brimming over with high spirits and happiness. These triumphs and joy of Kalo and Lekha are also shared by Biten who exaculates:

> "...you have triumphed over those others and over yourself.... Your story will be a legend of freedom, a legend to inspire and awaken."[21]

Thus Kalo and Chandralekha, taking risks as terrible as riding a tiger, rise high and deride the society which hates and insults them.

Bhattacharya's fourth novel *A Goddess Named Gold* contains characters who have bright vision of life. The book highlights some basic human values like real acts of kindness, self-sacrifice, freedom, friendship, goodness, purity, dignity, fight for the needy against the tyranny of the rich, etc.

The novelist shows Meera as a courageous girl not depressed and gloomy but possessing a positive attitude to life. Likewise, the profiteer Seth is portrayed as cheerful and hopeful all the time. The novelist expresses his belief in man's goodness which alone can root out malice and wrong through the words of the minstrel as:

> "Those who mock at goodness mock themselves; for, there is a secret goodness in them also."[22]

Bhattacharya emphasises the greatness and dignity of the downtrodden villagers who suffer a lot but not losing their honour and bright vision of future. The novelist expresses his belief that only through hard work and true love man can attain the betterment of life. The following remark of the minstrel made to the huge crowd of villagers towards the end of the novel is very significant:

> "The miracles will not drop upon us. It is we who have to create them with love and with sweat...."[23]

Through these words the listners are convinced that true touchstone is within one's grasp. So they are filled with new hope and feeling themselves released from a past, dead and gone, they visualise a bright future. Indeed, the novel reflects the novelist's optimism about the ultimate liquidation of all exploiters by the people.

Bhabani Bhattacharya's fifth novel, *Shadow from Ladakh*, reflects his affirmative vision of life. The need for the synthesis of modern industrialisation with small-scale rural industry, asceticism and non-violence, is hinted at in this novel through the synthesis of ideologies of Gandhigram and Steeltown, and through the love affairs of Bhashkar and Sumita. Thus all the frustrations and conflicts are calmed down to bring a new hopeful life.

Bhattacharya expresses his affirmation of life through: Suruchi's re-entering into a real life; Sumita's new love-affairs with Bhashkar overflowing with the true joy of life, Bhashkar's becoming joyous in getting rid of the sense of alienation; and Satyajit's becoming happier towards the close of the novel.

Again, the author highlights Tagore's belief in man's urge for happiness emanating from the fullness of life, and not from the attainment of riches through Satyajit. Satyajit always tries to make people understand and visualise an easier, freer and happier life. The book accentuates the Indian ideal of one basic goal—human happiness. All paths lead to it and their co-existence is highly necessary for man's acquiring the ideal of universal brotherhood. Bhattacharya points out that the raging brute in man can be overpowered only by the goodness of his inner spirit.

Bhattacharya portays Rupa as possessing new hope after her disappointment in first love. Similarly. Satyajit's renunciation is not a denial of the world. All characters show passion for life. Even the ascetic Sumita, giving up some of her asceticism, poses to be in love with life. Moreover, Bhattacharya emphasises the need for virtue, hard struggle and courage for achieving inner power and a happier life.

The author emphasises his point of argument that life is to be accepted in its totality. The novel concludes with Sumita's freedom from her father's strict aasceticism and enjoying her life's true fulfilment. Thus Bhattacharya's faith in the affirmative aspect of life is reflected in all his novels.

Bhabani Bhattacharya has denounced the negative implication of asceticism and self-abnegation in his various novels. In his *Music for Mohini* and *Shadow from Ladakh* he pleads for a full and joyous life by launching a vigorous campaign against the anti-life tendencies. In his latest novel *A Dream in Hawaii* he takes up a similar theme in which "an empty and sterile asceticism as well as mere animalism and unrestrained sexual hedonism are equally disparaged."[24]

Indeed, the novelist's concern in these three novels is about the truth of individual being.

In *Music for Mohini* Bhattacharya tries to communicate the Tagorean ideal that a man should live intensely and fully, seeking joy and beauty, and should not make life a penance or burden by imposing unnatural restraints and sacrifices on himself. There is juxtaposition of the forces of life and anti-life through Mohini. Her situation in relation to her husband's ideal is described as :

> "She had no ambitions to be Maitreyi: She hated serious study for which she had no patience. She needed life, feeling..... No one, by temperament could be less like Maitreyi."[25]

Mohini thinks that a woman has to live like a woman. She has jest for life and loves laughter and music. But she is to make adjustment in the Big House. Jayadev has a dual personality struggling in himself. Describing his predicament the novelist aptly remarks:

> "A man closer to life, more attuned to reality, would have achieved an inner balance with little strain, fulfilling the claims of both his mind and art. But Jayadev, detached from the world, shrank from life, afraid of his own awakened spirit with its needs and demands."[26]

The conflict reaches its culmination when Mohini makes the journey to the Devi's shrine with her mother-in-law followed by the confrontation between Jayadev and his mother where Jayadev rejects the anti-life forces of the world by saying:

> "Values, Mother! There are values beyond your grasp, since you'll always try to reach them with your reason, never with your feelings.... Blind belief shapes your thinking; blind belief cannot make a sentiment."[27]

And through this rejection Jayadev also frees himself. The resolution of the conflict takes place through Mohini's pregnancy followed by her adjustment with her mother-in-law. Thus Bhattacharya denounces the negative implication of asceticism and self-abnegation in order to achieve a full and joyous life.

In *Shadow from Ladakh* Bhattacharya expresses the Tagorean idea of the acceptance of life in its totality by avoiding unnatural restraints and sacrifices on man that make life a penance or burden. This idea is expressed through the poet's words:

> "It is fullness of life that makes one happy, not fullness of possessions."[28]

The symbolic marriage of Steeltown and Gandhigram in the persons of Bhashkar and Sumita, or Satyajit's return to a balanced life show that Bhattacharya rejects the Gandhian economy and the Gandhian Brahmacharya. Suruchi breaks her bangles in pain and anger when Satyajit speaks to her about his wish to observe Brahmacharya. Since a woman has to live like a woman Suruchi says: "An ascetic woman is a contradiction in terms." In fact, Satyajit denies his wife a life of fulfilment. He expects her to become a wife like Kasturba to her Gandhi. But since her submission is not whole-hearted; she admires the girl, Jhanak, for her courage to live as her natural instincts prompt her to live. She knows the need of life of every girl and so she wants her daughter Sumita shed off her Satyajitism.

Satyajit's friend Bireswar tells Satyajit to surrender himself to Suruchi to feel once again the beauty and joy of life. Now Satyajit realises his own mistakes. Actually, experience dictates him to begin a new life of "dynamic equilibrium" after his fast. This situation is described thus:

> "Suruchi was an urge for him to live, relive and not on the Gandhian plane. His newly won release would seek expression in the honest acceptance of every human need."[29]

Nandini says that Sumita's asceticism is a negation of life because all her natural instincts have been suppressed by it. Nandini demonstrates the power of love as one of the noblest of human emotions. She warns Sumita by saying that one day the terrific wave of love will seize her too. Right at the end of the novel Sumita is seized by this wave. Now she begins a new life. The novelist describes this situation thus:

> "Satyajit, held his daughter no longer in his relentless power!
>
> She was free, free at last."[30]

Concluding the novel with this liberation of Sumita the novelist highlights the theme of life versus anti-life forces siding himself with life since he denounces negative implication of asceticism and self-abnegation of the protagonist.

In *A Dream in Hawaii* Bhattacharya denounces the negative implication of asceticism and self-abnegation through the character of the protagonist Swami Yogananda. When the Swami is standing on the beach of Waikiki clad in the robes of renunciation, he sees a well-endowed maiden, lying in her brief bathing suit, smearing herself with sun tan lotion. Swami Yogananda is enchanted because it is the first time in his life to see a woman in the full beauty of bareness. This sight gives the Swami sensuous pleasure as a surprise and a shock. Swami Yogananda's predicament here is not sex but honesty since the honest acceptance of every human need, the motto of Bhattacharya, finds its expression in him.

The novelist censures asceticism and intellectualistic ideals because they call for an unhealthy repression of human desires and emotions which stifles creativity. Actually, Neeloy Mukherjee cannot submerge his identity completely into that of Swami Yogananda, a role imposed on him by Devjani, his student paramour in Benares. But when he achieves fame and success as a Swami he realises the truth of his inner being which continues to be Neeloy, surviving against all outward impositions and control. Swami Yogananda brings back his own consciousness of Neeloy at the end of the hovel. His journey back to his ashram after Sylvia Koo has awakened the dormant Neeloy in him is a journey of self-realisation. Thus Bhattacharya emphasises the need to be honest to one's inner being by denouncing the negative implication of asceticism and self abnegation.

REFERENCES

1. K.K. Sharma, *Bhabani Bhattacharya: His Vision and Themes* (New Delhi: Abhinav Publications, 1979), 13.
2. Bhabani Bhattacharya: *So Many Hungers!* (Bombay: Jaico Publishing House, 1964), 1.

3. *So Many Hungers!* 9.
4. *So Many Hungers!* 176.
5. *So Many Hungers!* 22.
6. *So Many Hungers!* 111.
7. *So Many Hungers!* 25.
8. Harish Raizada, *Bhabani Bhattacharya—The Novelist of Social Ferment;* quoted in "Response: Recent Revelations of Indian Fiction in English," (ed.) Hari Mohan Prasad (Bareilly: Prakash Book Depot. 1983), 127.
9. *So Many Hungers*! 120.
10. *So Many Hungers*! 127.
11. *So Many Hungers*! 143.
12. *So Many Hungers*! 156.
13. *So Many Hungers*! 214-15.
14. K.K. Sharma 26.
15. Bhabani Bhattacharya, *Music for Mohini* (New Delhi: An Orient Paperback, 1952), 94.
16. *Music for Mohini* 189.
17. *Music for Mohini* 188.
18. *Music for Mohini* 188.
19. Bhabani Bhattacharya, *He Who Rides a Tiger* (Delhi: An Orient Paperback, Hind Pocket Books (P) Ltd., 1955), 219.
20. *He Who Rides a Tiger* 231.
21. *He Who Rides a Tiger* 232.
22. Bhabani Bhattacharya, *A Goddess Named Gold* (Delhi: Hind Pocket Books (P) Ltd., 1967), 63.
23. *A Goddess Named Gold* 303.
24. Bhagawat S. Goyal, *The Sensuous and the Sublime: Bhabani Bhattacharya's —A Dream in Hawaii* quoted in "Perspectives on Bhabani Bhattacharya" (ed.) R.K. Srivastava (Ghaziabad: Vimal Prakashan, 1982), 180.
25. *Music for Mohini* (New Delhi: An Orient Paperback, 1952), 104-5.
26. *Music for Mohini* (Bombay: Jayco, 1964), 151.
27. *Music for Mohini* (Bombay: Jayco, 1964), 180.
28. Bhabani Bhattacharya: *Shadow From Ladakh* (Delhi: Hind Pocket Books, Ltd., 1966), 14.
29. *Shadow From Ladakh* 353.
30. *Shadow From Ladakh* 359.

6

BHABANI BHATTACHARYA'S STYLE

Bhabani Bhattacharya is a great innovator and a free user of the English language for artistic purposes. He carried out experiments in English language and has produced his own variety of style to depict the racy speech of Indian peasant masses about whom he writes in his novels. In order to be able to convey Indian sensibilities and culture he has used an Indianised style with traces of Indianisms in it. In this he has made a vista of necessity since his Bengali phrases and idioms do interfere with his English. The following study will show some of the stylistic devices used by Bhattacharya with a close attention to the striking features in his individual use of language and narrative technique recurrent in his novels.

A recurrent feature in Bhattacharya's language is his use of literal translation of phrases, idioms or proverbs into English from Indian languages, especially Bengali. He literally translates proverbs reflecting the Indian way of life and the typical Indian outlook on life. The homeliness and aptness of Indian proverbs used by the novelist and their intelligibility to the non-Indian reader are shown, for example, by the following list of proverbs collected from his different novels:

From *So Many Hungers*!

(1) The elephant lays the road for a rat (New Delhi: Orient Paperback, 1978, 62).

(2) A rat slips in through a doorway too narrow for the bulky elephant.

(3) Money is a winged bird. It will fly off (62).

(4) Through their fingers money goes pouring like water (129).

From *Music for Mohini*

(1) Can the tongue relish rice and fish, can the eyelids close in peace while there is a maiden daughter in the house? (Bombay: Jaico, 1964, 42).

(2) They're like the tomcat who became an ascetic when he was too old and cripple to run after rats (47).

(3) Horses and camels find the stream bottomless, but the rat squeaks (64).

(4) You may be digging a canal from the river to your house door and inviting the crocodile (44 and 75).

(5) The tail of a cow and the tongue of a rustic never cease wagging (83).

(6) To a lotus pool the wary jeweller goes and values the white blooms with his test-stone (104).

(7) How can a plum tree grow pears? (158)

From *He Who Rides a Tiger*

(1) You think you are not getting sixteen annas for your silver rupee (Delhi: Hind Pocket Books, 1955, 132).

(2) People have long tongues and tongues will wag (172).

(3) It was proper that a well-wisher be told what is cooking in your pot (Bombay: Jaico, 1955, 186).

From *A Goddess Named Gold*

(1) A thousand moustaches can live together in amity but not four breasts (Delhi: Hind Pocket Books, 1960, 42).

(2) Money will buy even the milk of a tigress (53).

(3) A duck must swim and a rat must steal grain (108).

(4) When an ant grows wings and starts flying in the air it is not far from its doom (128).

(5) The two who sit on the same bough of a tree cannot hack off the bough (162).

(6) You may clutch at the touchstone as a drowning person reaches for a twig in the current (176).

(7) A baby snake wanting to eat a python (190).

(8) When an ass laments the loss of a cow, his guts will not pine for five drops of milk (191).

(9) A good mango tree hides its crop of fruit behind thick leaves (199).

(10) A goat grows horns but does not become an antelope (249).

From *Shadow from Ladakh*

(1) One must wear painted plumes in the company of peacocks (Delhi: Hind Pocket Books, 1966, 112).

These literal translations give to his English the flavour of his native language. They clearly represent an attempt to give individuality to the characters and to mark their Indianness. Regarding Bhattacharya's purposeful use of these proverbs K.R. Chandrasekharan fittingly remarks:

> "Their use may be considered as a successful linguistic experiment because they introduce local colour without reducing intelligibility. As a rule the proverbs fit the characters who use them."[1]

Commenting on the novelist's successful use of these expressions for their unmistakable flavour of the vernacular speech R.K. Srivastava remarks as follows:

> "They also provide a glimpse of the wise sayings of the rural people preserved and transmitted in their everyday conversation, as also their attitude to life, and, above all, are gentle reminder to the reader that the characters are firmly rooted in the Indian soil."[2]

Bhattacharya also indulges in the coinage of new compound words by literally translating words, phrases and sometimes whole sentences from the regional languages. Among such small phrases and compound words which look exotic in English writing we may mention individual words, for example: *cook-woman, cinema-play, picture-play, water-machine* (for water tap), *cook-shop, well-water, child-pain, happy-sad-mother, mother of Onu, tear-haze, picture-show* (cinema), *fire-wagon* (train), *flower-bed* (bridal bed), *head-protector* (umbrella), *chatter-machine* (radio), *joy-moments, tongue-clever, milk-infant, day-down* (sun-set), *tying a soul to the sari end, laughing a bellyful, eating one's salt, eating one's head, holding one's chin up,* etc.

Bhattacharya also uses expressions reflecting the attitude of the traditional rural people in matters of measurement or counting. When Meera's age is referred to as 'ten-eleven' and the position of the sun in the sky is referred to as 'a bare man-height' the traditional rural people's belief in proximity due to the lack of their education, but not in precision and accuracy is clearly revealed. Besides these, the novelist uses a large number of phrases literally translated from Bengali to English and some of them have parallel phrases in other North Indian languages. *So Many Hungers*! abounds in such phrases. Some of them are: *white as lime plaster; greed in the belly; full upto the throat; sun-wet-face; shame bit into her; just a way of talk,* etc.

In *Music for Mohini* we see such phrases: *Get this plain fact in your stomach; Eat my head; A cheekful of smile; Anger bit into her,* etc. Again, *A Goddess Named Gold* also abounds in such examples: *Two men-lengths; Move your buttocks faster; One of our skin and sweet,* etc.

Bhattacharya also makes use of abusive epithets of colloquial nature like: *brother of a bug; brother of a cockroach; brother of a mule; brother of a hawk; sisters of a vixen; son of a pig; son of a crab; son of an ass; son of a crocodile; son of a city peacock,* etc.

The novelist also coins diminutives which are distinctly based on Bengali idioms like: *childling, ghostling, frogling, wifeling, godling, youngling, starvelling.* etc. in proper contexts. Thus, native idioms are employed to enrich the resources of English. Use of heavy alliteration is also one of the prominent features of Bhattacharyan style. Examples are: *Ranjan in a rush* (in *Music for Mohini*), *Monju in a muse* (in *So Many Hungers!*). But the alliteration is deliberate in these cases. *Heritage of hate* and *bonefire of boats*, etc. are also other examples of Bhattacharya striving after effect by rhetorical means.

The novelist also takes up the device of reduplication of word with a change of initial sound to produce a characteristic Bengali effect with dubious success. They are like: *Vote-mote* for 'vote' and *board-moard* for 'board' in *A Goddess Named Gold*. It is difficult to understand what artistic effect is gained by this linguistic obscurity. This stylistic device is an example of the licence Bhattacharya took with English grammar. In order to suggest the ways of folk speech, Bhattacharya literally translates its picturesque expressions like: *ships of the sky* (for aeroplanes); *the wonder ray* (for x-ray); *a speaking wire* (for telephone); *song machine* (for gramophone), *windvan* (for motorcar), etc. These, however, are more justifiable than *vote-mote* and *board-moard*.

To suit the mentality of the rural character Bhattacharya uses a large number of Bengali and Hindi words like: *apsara, asirbad, bhai, beta, bhootni, chal, champa, choorie, dal, dhoti, dak-qhar, dilruba, dakini, ghee, haat, jilebi, kachu, kajal, kabiraj, kos, kamar, kusa, laddoo, nimkin, pronam, puri, palki, shehnai, sindur, swarga* and *thana*, etc. Besides these, the novelist also uses many other Indian words having their English equivalents like: *ma-bap* (mother-father); *Viman* (aerial car); *Brahmastra* (wonder-missile); *pagla-ghanta* (crazy bell); chamar (untouchable); *tamasha* (spectacle); *lota-kambal* (water-bowl and blanket); *ojha* (exorcist); etc.

There are plenty of onomatopoeic words not conveying special kind of meaning and significance in the novels of Bhattacharya. When these words are not italicised in the texts, they cause an irritation to the readers. Because the readers are confused in the absence of the annotations, whether these words belong to English or some other language. Some of them are *khitir-mitir, doog-doog* (sounds of drum); *shup-shup* (sound of a book); *hukka-huahua* (cry of a jackal); *mush-mush* (sounds of shoes); *jhinn* (chirp of crickets); *clop-clop* (sounds of sendals); *thoo-thoo* (sounds of spitting); *hen-hen-hen* (laughter); *khit-khit* (useless talk); *phut-phutti* (motor bike); etc. These are only examples of Bhattacharya's ridiculous propensities in the use of English.

Bhattacharya also uses many English words which are taken as Indian words due to distortion and wide use. They are frequently used even by the illiterate people. So their misspellings conform to their use by the rustics. There are some such words: *Engreze, Chinee, Japanee, Iranee, Gorement, Sigrette* etc.

Another stylistic device Bhattacharya takes up in his writings is his formation of interrogative sentences by adding a note of interrogation at the end of assertive sentences. In such sentences the rising tone of the speaker behind the interrogation mark implies question whereas the level or lowered tone indicates a statement or an answer. Examples are: *You are wed, Kajoli*?; *This is the groom*?; *Father is well*?; *Because of you he fled*?; *Good shoes*?; *You are pleased, Onu*?; *This village has suffered much*?; etc.

A prominent practice of Bhattacharya's style is his formation of adjectival forms by adding the suffix *ful* to nouns even when they do not become idiomatic. Examples are: *skyful, fistful, prideful, palmsful, cheekful,* etc. Bhattacharya also uses the method of calling the name of the implement for a workman and the name of the article for a merchant. It is shown by his use of the term *Halwai* or *sweetshop* for a merchant selling sweet meats.

A remarkable feature of Indianness in Bhattacharya's style is his use of words like; *han, hoon. arey, nah, beta, beti, bhai, bahen, pan, taveez,* etc. He uses them for making local colour in the speech of the rustics who do not speak English. Sometimes he uses expression like: *Eat my head.* Employment of these words serves no useful purpose according to Chandrasekharan. But R.K. Srivastava states that use of such words serves as a periodic reminder of the nationality and the mother language of the character. Dr. Mrs. Meenakshi Mukherjee remarks:

> "It is difficult to see what is gained by this simple substitution, except perhaps as a reminder that the characters are not speaking in English."[3]

Another prominent feature in Bhattacharya's style is his significant use of words and phrases repeatedly to impress the reader. There are many sentences used recurrently in different contexts. One such instance is: "I know a man by the look in his face." The policeman arresting Kalo for stealing banana uses it for Kalo. Rajani, the procurer, thinking Kalo to be his fit assistance, uses the same remark and Motichand also uses it to Kalo in disguise at the temple. Again, "We've got to hit back," is another sentence used repeatedly as a refrain in the novel. Emphasising on the purposeful use of such refrains by Bhattacharya K.R. Chandrasekharan remarks:

> "Bhattacharya deliberately and carefully uses such verbal refrains and echoes because "he is conscious of the power of words to suggest the tone or to induce states of feeling."[4]

In *Shadow from Ladakh* also the novelist uses "a terrific wave" as a refrain in many occasions by different characters. Again, on a number of occasions in *A Goddess Named Gold* and *Shadow from Ladakh* Bhattacharya uses the Gandhian expression, "to wipe every tear from every eye" (first used by Gandhi in his mission in Naokhali).

Bhattacharya often drops the 'to be' verb to echo Bengali idiom. He also uses short disjointed sentences for the same effect: "Why speak? What use! Trees and rocks have a heart. Not man. Why speak?" But as Mrs. Mukherjee comments, this is no way to write naturally in English. Frequent altering of the basic sentence patterns of English makes the language violated. His device of putting an interrogation mark, as shown earlier somewhere in this chapter, after a statement of fact to make it a question does not sound good English style. Some more examples are: "You play tennis? You dance?" (*Music for Mohini,* 43).

A remarkable feature of Bhattacharya's style is his telling use of irony. Prominent examples are given below: In *So Many Hungers!* Kajoli thinks that "the soldiers are all kindness." But the same kind soldier rapes her and flees from her. Again, Kajoli decides to sell her body to the procuress to keep her brother and mother alive. The same night her mother also decides to commit suicide. So she has left her tattered sari behind for Kajoli's use and has worn a piece of gunny-cloth. It is in a corner of this gunny cloth that Kajoli has tied up her ill-earned money which will maintain her family.

Again, in *Music for Mohini* the names of English people, such as, White Leather, Miss Coffin and Miss Stiff have a tinge of irony. Although Sudha discloses to Jayadev, all about Mohini's plan of offering blood, to win advantage for herself, Jayadev is unaware of her sinister intentions and says: "How good of her to come, rushing to tell him. He was grateful." Sudha sees Mohini and Jayadev, journeying to Calcutta by a bullock-cart. Her intense feeling of triumph and achievement is described thus: "Her body tensed with bitter pleasure and her small delicate fists clutched the iron bars of the window." The irony here is that she loses the battle for the Big House while she thinks she wins.

Another instance of irony is seen in *He Who Rides a Tiger* and it is when the magistrate, who had questioned the worth of Kalo's life, comes to touch Kalo's feet when the latter disguises as Mangal Adhikari. Another instance of irony is when the grateful blacksmith Viswanath tells Mangal Adhikari (blacksmith Kalo disguised as a Brahmin): "So long as there are true hearted Brahmins like you...."

In *A Goddess Named Gold* also there is instance of irony when the Seth compares himself with the minstrel in not caring for money while the reader knows his care for money. The dialogue between the minstrel and the Seth is ironic. The Seth pretends to be very poor and regrets that he has not enough money to lend to all the poor people who "are hungry for cash and more cash." But the minstrel replies: "Sethji, yours is a dedicated life."

One important aspect of Bhattacharya's style is his sense of humour. The opening chapter of *Music for Mohini* provides scope for delicate humour with Heeralal and Mohini's teasing each other by literally translating their names into English. Even their studies present humorous scene. When their father unexpectedly enters the room, Heeralal poses to do arithmetic with a broken pencil and Mohini pretends to study *Ancient India* while in reality she is reading the novel *The Poisoned Kiss.* There is also a humorous scene when Mohini's mother-in-law wants her to wear a costly stud on the nose by piercing it. But to save herself through a trick she tells the Mother that her nose has been vowed away to the goddess Kali by her grandmother to get rid of cold. We agree with R.K. Srivastava who writes:

> "*He Who Rides a Tiger* is written in a light-veined style full of pleasantries and exaggerations and spiced with irony, which make his other linguistic experiments palatable."[5]

A glimpse of sardonic humour is seen when Motichand asks Lekha whether he should buy or sell. Confused and perplexed by this question, Lekha mechanically repeats the words, "Buy...sell," So Motichand rushes to his office to buy first. Luckily he makes huge profits thereby and thus causes the strangest thing. Bhattacharya's comic vein is also discernible in his use of imagery to criticise a character. He laughs at Motichand by saying: "a man whose big nose seemed to rest on an enormous moustache in a long goatlike face."

In *Shadow from Ladakh* we see a humorous description of anti-Chinese demonstration in Delhi during the time of Chinese invasion in India. The description shows a mock-funeral procession of common men organised to signify the death of friendship between the two countries. Bhattacharya uses Indian ways of speaking and Indian words, especially Bengali, at many judicious contexts for artistic value which he attains easily in his novels. In fact, Bhattacharya shows neither an excessive fondness for Indianisms nor does he unnecessarily elevate his narration and description.

One remarkable feature in Bhattacharyan writings is his use of homely and natural dialogues typical of rural life. Dialogues, comprising of idioms and phrases, proverbs and sayings, similes and metaphors, are used to reflect the rural conversation. Here is one instance from *Music for Mohini* in the dialogue of Old Mother, Heeralal and Mohini:

> Old Mother went on: "Can the tongue relish rice and fish, can the eyelids close in peace while there is a maiden daughter in the house?"
>
> "And she shooting up like a palm-tree!" added Heeralal, recalling a talk in low tones between his elders which he overheard.
>
> Mohini stood up and leaned against Father's desk.
>
> "Grandmother, see how the mischievous monkey nags me. Why is he such a busybody? Why does he not fry his own fish and leave me alone?"
>
> She stuck one end of Father's fat penholder, scarred by her previous nibblings, between her teeth.
>
> "You wait," Heeralal warned, "We'll forget you the moment you cross our doorsill."[6]

Bhattacharya is a good user of metaphorical expressions in his dialogues and narration to reflect rural people and their life.

One instance of such metaphorical speech is seen in *Music for Mohini* from the mouth of the Old Mother? "You will brighten another house, child. What use is a lamp, golden and filled with oil, if it has no wick? The house is the lamp, man is like oil, the woman is the wick Mohini; and happiness the living flame" (39). Again, in *He Who Rides a Tiger* Kalo's warning to Lekha about Viswanath is metaphorical: "We stand on the edge of a cliff. A hundred eyes keep watch on us, waiting to see if we slip and fall. We have to be wary," and also, "the counterfeit coin needed more glitter than the real" (112).

Indeed, there is a progression of metaphorical expression from crudity and rough edges in *So Many Hungers*! to sophistication and dignity in *Shadow from Ladakh*. In the first novel, the novelist uses crude metaphors like: "His ideas had been shaped on the anvil of reason" (42). But in his later novel, his metaphor is poetic and symbolic. Such expression can be seen when he writes about Bhashkar:

> "In the years past he had gone from experience to experience, all inhibitions cast aside, as free in feelings as a western man, and it had been worth-while indeed. But after a time a queer discontent had come. He was, he thought, journeying from exhaustion to exhaustion. Moments that lived briefly, futilely mounting from day to day, year to year. It was as though he had been scribbling on a sheet of paper with a pen dipped in clear water—the curious image came to his mind—the water dried and the words were gone."[7]

Bhattacharya also uses repetitive and fragmentary sentences without connectives or verbs or adjectives or subjects and no subordinate clauses to convey the feverish inhuman drama of businessmen forcing to have their pound of flesh from the agonised war victims of the country.

One instance in *Music for Mohini* is:

> "High premium? Buy at a high premium. See it go

> higher, higher. Thirty per cent. Fifty per cent. Hundred per cent dividend. Dividend to make death machine. Scrap-iron hurled from projectiles, a million tons a month. A million deaths a month. Death into dividend. Death into dividend (19).

The various features of style shown above show the artistic maturity of Bhattacharya's writing. His style is not static but undergoing a process of development. Starting with a crude and crippled style in *So Many Hungers!* Bhattacharya improves his mastery over the language in *Music for Mohini* which reflects ironic speeches and natural dialogues of the rural people with abundance of comic spirit and images. In *He Who Rides a Tiger* there is an equal proportion of comic vein and irony. It has smooth and consistent literally translated words and phrases with the missing of long descriptions and graphic details. In *A Goddess Named Gold* there is a striking use of images and irony; and humour also becomes predominant here. Using shorter dialogues the style becomes lighter in flow. In this regard we agree with R.K. Srivastava's remark:

> "Bhattacharya seems to be driving a bullockcart and is occasionally diverted by concerns such as showing the rural side, portraying the behaviour and speech of the traditional people—an irresistible temptation—and the result is the uneven pace of his narrative."[8]

Bhattacharya's style shows a distinct sign of maturity in *Shadow from Ladakh.* The flow of the style runs smoothly ringing with political, scientific, military terms and with reverberating slogans, such as: *Hindi-Chini bhai bhai* reflecting the synthesis of the ideologies of Gandhi, Tagore, Buddha and Nehru.

In his last novel *A Dream in Hawaii* his style becomes plain, devoid of similes and metaphors. It is not as dignified and elevated as that of *Shadow from Ladakh.* So once again, we agree with R.K. Srivastava's fitting remark:

> "It is as if after the ebb and flow, the ocean has calmed down. For once the style has the fusion of the East and the West—simple expressions with colloquial terms from the West. Bhattacharya has no taboos as if he were dreaming where exhibitions don't exist—a sort of fitting finale—so far—to the writing work of nearly four decades."[9]

BHATTACHARYA'S AUTHENTIC TONE, INDIANNESS AND POPULARITY

Bhattacharya has an authentic tone in all his novels. He conveys Indian sensibility and Indian culture to his readers with this authentic tone. The choice of common theme, the employment of traditional technique and the adoption of a special stylistic pattern and device of language used by the Indian masses in all his novels show his Indianness.

Bhabani Bhattacharya is a mature creative Indo-Anglian fictionist-cum-critic. He has his own theory of fiction. All his novels are written to conform to this theory of fiction. He speaks with authentic tone in all his novels which are all reflections of contemporary Indian life and culture. He has a great admiration for the spiritual and cultural heritage of India. His cultural awareness constitutes his Indianness and it conforms to Prof. V.K. Gokak's definition of Indianness of an Indian writer:

> "An Indian, then, is a person who owns up the entire Indian heritage and not merely a portion of it. This integral cultural awareness is an indispensable feature of Indianness."[10]

Bhattacharya's depth and range of sensibility and experience, but not his philosophy, are the things that mould his expression of Indianness. Indeed, his tone of language and mode of expression conform to the theory propounded by Gokak:

> "The extent of Indianness of work of art will depend upon the intensity and manifoldness with which an Indian writer responds to this tradition and recreates it in his own consciousness."[11]

Bhabani Bhattacharya, really, has the necessary inwardness to write on Indian traditions and cultures to create a permanent work of art. Although he writes in an alien language he is not losing the grasp of Indian sensibility under the impact of this language. In fact, he has not alienated from the Indian social, religious and political milieu. And in this regard Prof. S.C. Sanyal's remark is worth close attention:

> "The authenticity and honesty of Indo-Anglian writers is beyond criticism. They state how they have been in the Indian milieu and write about their experiences of today's Indian society without losing the national identity."[12]

Bhattacharya is a reputed Indo-Anglian novelist who has been constantly aiming at an Indianness bereft of temporal and spatial values in his novels. He has various experiments giving English a distinctively Indian tone and colouring without doing violence to its basic linguistic structure. His such practice deserves credit and special appreciation. Bhattacharya has not only possessed the thought and imagery, idiom and consciousness of his own country's milieu, but also has transformed, with his personal experience, the material into literature that is universal in its artistic appeal. He projects a very Indian image in his novels in which characters behave in ways that are recognised as 'Indians' by Western scholars and critics and by every foreigner. What characterises the Indianness in his writing is actually in mind, his soul behind the organisation of the content, his life attitudes and modes of perception. Rooted in the native soil, his writing struggles to cope with the spirit of the modern world and puts forth its own peculiar fruit. In this connection Samares C. Sanyal quotes Bhattacharya himself who remarks:

> "The fruit bearing has not just been traditional…a writer cannot live without roots. An Indian writer deeply concerned with the lives of the people cannot get transplanted from the earth of centuries-old traditions despite full exposer to alien influences…."[13]

Really speaking, Bhattacharya has had strong exposure to winds from other shores so that the fruit bearing has not just been traditional, while his roots remain intact. In spite of the presence of this outside consciousness, prominently due to the novelist's use of an alien medium of expression, his writing is not parasitic literature and his novels are not devoid of Indianness. This fact is supported by the following remark:

> "In Indo-Anglian writing mostly both the theme and the treatment have been suffused by the genesis of our racial culture while the medium of expression remained alien."[14]

Since Bhattacharya is a creative Indo-Anglian novelist, he writes on whatever aspects of life he chooses to write about with grasp and thoroughness. In all his novels he deals with a number of themes (all rooted on the cultural and social heritage of India) such as: "the horrors of war and famine, pestilence, clash of traditions, ignorance, misguided faith in religion, superstitions, casteism and economic and food crisis."[15] In fact, Bhattacharya recognises "Man" in relation to society and as such he portrays poverty; hunger and disease; the sufferings of the innumerable poor; tradition and modernity; social evils and tensions; inter-racial relations; changing values of modern civilisation; crisis of character; East-West cultural contact, etc.

All the first five novels of Bhattacharya are set against Indian social scene in the perspective of world-shaking historical events whereas the latest and sixth novel has its setting both in India and America's Hawaii island and deals with the theme of spiritual quest. Thus Bhattacharya chooses whatever aspect of life as his theme and treats it with his artistic grasp and thoroughness. Being a creative artist-cum-critic Bhattacharya presents a vivid image of Indian life which is the result of his deep involvement in life and criticises the cruelties and inhuman acts of the anti-social and anti-democratic forces of contemporary India. To show how he depicts Indian life, culture, superstition and belief, especially of the Bengalis, we may deal with each one of his novels one by one.

The first novel *So Many Hungers!* vividly depicts Indian life and problems. It depicts the two devils of war and famine which squeeze the blood of human race. Of the two, famine is the worse because it keeps man neither completely dead nor alive. The rich people trade on the helpless victims of poverty, ignorance and illiteracy and feed on the miseries of the people. Hunger was the fate, an expiation of the sins of past lives of the poor people. The government would not feed them whereas they should feed the government. The famine was artificial. It was not a natural calamity but was the result of man's cruelty. When all the uprooted people were pauperised inflated currency gave a finishing touch to the tragedy.

The novel presents the inhuman and cold attitude of the administrators and the vicious and corrupted atmosphere of Bengal's economy. The scene is described by the novelist thus:

> "Corruption had grown like an epidemic and money had become a mad-hunger. Never in the land's history had the process that made the rich richer, the poor poorer, gained such ruthless intensity. The authority took little heed and set it aside as a passing phenomenon. But the poor suffered untold misery and the end of one tale was the beginning of another."[16]

The novel presents a deep emotional tone through its heart-rending scenes. Many peasants migrate to Calcutta and they die in the streets. The readers' sense of humanity is shocked by the scenes where a jackal perches on the thigh of a pregnant woman and tears at her swollen belly while her screams slash the air, where Kishore becomes the victim of circumstances, where mass arrest is done consequent upon Quit India Resolution and where Kajoli is raped by a soldier.

One remarkable aspect of Indian rural life shown in the

novel is that the villagers are bound by the sense of oneness, common brotherhood, sharing the weal and woe of one by another. Through the character of Devesh Basu is shown the villagers' devotion, hero-worship and their motto of living and dying together.

The novel depicts the villagers' belief in the omens, their superstitions, customs, traditions, convictions, etc. There is also reference to Indian people's devotion and love for the monumental epics—the *Ramayana* and the *Bhagavata*. The worship of the cow Mangala shows an evidence of the villagers' love for a cow as a mother. There is also depiction of the spirit of sacrifice which is inherent in the blood and veins of rural folk through Kajoli's mother's offering of cow to the fisherwoman. Bhattacharya neatly portrays Indian people's belief in the predestined lot of man, the inscrutable Fate and unmodifiable Destiny. Moreover, there are references to many customs and beliefs of the rural folk such as—a woman's drawing her sari over her face whenever a stranger comes, washing the stranger's feet after a journey, worshipping of the sacred Tulsi plant and the dusk-Goddess, the blowing of conch as a sign of good omen and happiness, the chanting of the sacred names of 'Rama' and 'Hanumana' to frighten and drive out the ghosts and demons, etc.

Through the character and activities of Rahoul the novelist clearly delineates the advancement of science in the then Indian society. Hunger strikes, political rallies; agitations and processions are revealed to be the means used by the poor and exploited people for sensing and shocking the rich class. Through these means of the poor class Bhattacharya propounds his social theory of mutual recognition of human beings by human beings.

The second novel *Music for Mohini* presents a cross section of the contemporary Indian society full of superstitions and irrational orthodoxy. The novelist describes the society thus:

"Society, rural society (and nine-tenths of India was

> rural) was sick with taboos and inhibitions of its own making; the iniquities of caste and untouchability; the ritualism that passed for religion; the wide flung cobweb of superstitious faith."[17]

We see the cruel nature of the ritual pattern of the past through the advice of Jayadeva's mother to Mohini to offer a part of her living breast to the Virgin Goddess to bear a child. Bhattacharya aims at bringing a social renaissance by removing the dead conventions from the core of Indian social life. These conventions are: mothers' objection to their daughters' going to school for education, their insistence on early marriage, their faith in the horoscopes and matching of the eight signs of luck, the tragedy of the malefic conjunction of the stars, the belief in astrology, wearing the amulet round the neck to ward off evil, etc.

The novel pictures the tradition of marriage alliances through matrimonial columns of newspapers. There is the depiction of the conflict between the Indian ways of life and Westernised outlook through the wrath of the old Mother at the indecent questions posed at the marriage interviews of Mohini. The practice of believing in the personality of astrologer is revealed through the portrait of fortune teller Govind Ram.

The observance of the austerities during marriage functions, the existence of joint family system in Hindu society, the chanting of Sanskrit Mantras in religious and marriage ceremonies, the restraint of food to a Hindu wife before her husband, dedication of evening meal to the Goddess Kali and eating nothing after sun set are penned with matchless power in the novel. The novel depicts scriptural belief on the necessity of the birth of a son for salvation of the father and for carrying down the family name for another span of life on earth. The birth of a child under a particular star and the arrival of a daughter-in-law or cattle too are taken to have their effects, good or bad, on the inmates of the family. The existence of four castes systems in Behula, the preference of Ayurveda to the Western allopathic medicines are vividly depicted in the novel.

The restriction of marriage of any girl under sixteen, restriction of widow re-marriage and the existence of untouchability in the society are shown to be passing through a process of change. Indeed, the end of the novel presents an amalgam of the best of the old and the best of the modern along with the best of the village and the best of the city by weeding out all the evil overgrowths on the social life of the people of Behula.

The third novel *He Who Rides a Tiger* depicts contemporary Indian life rooted on the degrading political and economic system in the caste-ridden society. the central character Kalo's protest against the rich class represents the moral protest of the real people of the time. The novel vividly portrays caste-sanctimoniousness, the Brahminic ways of life, the smug hypocrisy of the local rich, the human cruelty and emotional disfigurement under the degraded economy of the land. The novelist presents many contrasts—property and poverty, goodness and hypocrisy, power and helplessness. The novel depicts the existence of superstitions in that age of science and technology, the role of tradition and religion, the unconquerable state of one's conscience, the sociological obsessions and psychological clashes of individuals, the trading on the flesh of the poor and the helpless and the dividing of superiority and inferiority complexes.

The novel reveals man's living on hope. As long as hope remains man exists and when hope leaves man it is the end of his life. Adhering to this optimistic idea Kalo thinks of making a living in the city. Bhattacharya depicts convent schools imparting better standard of education. There is also reference to the monopoly of education by the rich class only. There are also references to Western man's discovering the buried secrets of ancient India's arms and weapons such as: the *Viman* (aerial car) battling from above the cloud cover; the *Subdavedhi* (arrow flying to a target by sound); the *Sammohanastra* (a wonder missile burstling and releasing a mist for putting a whole army to sleep).

The novelist depicts the institution of prostitution prevalent in the then Indian society. Sometimes men are seen disguised as Brahmins by wearing saffron loin cloth, smearing the body with ashes and marking a red-paste trident of Shiva on their forehead to make a living by begging in the streets. Such men can hoodwink even the rich men to accept them as Yogis with great spiritual power. The novel presents Indian people's belief in the scriptural customs and rites. But it also shows rich man with no time or heart for prayer and penance. The excommunication of the untouchables, taking Shivaratri to be the most sacred day in the year, the theories of re-incarnation and Avatars and man's enjoying the bitter fruit of retribution for a crime committed in the past life are vividly presented.

The novelist refers to the superiority of the Brahmin class and the Hindu law which does not permit divorce. The novel hopefully presents the vision of a democratic India. Lastly, it also presents the spirit of freedom flowing through the veins and arteries of every man and woman including the prisoners who shout the reverberant slogans "'Quit India' and 'Jai Hind'—'Victory to India.'"

The fourth novel *A Goddess Named Gold* reflects a vivid picture of the contemporary Indian village society. It reflects the villagers' united moral supremacy over the selfishness of the Seths and the landlords. The novel reflects the novelist's resplendent vision of life. He highlights basic human values like—acts of kindness, self-sacrifice, freedom, friendship, purity, dignity, fight for the needy against the oppression of the rich, etc. The novelist also emphasises on the need for the political and social reformations.

One aspect of Indian village life depicted in the novel is the existence of profiteers and black-marketeers. It depicts the real significance of freedom through the symbolism of amulet worn by Meera. Greed, jealousy and selfishness are depicted to be inherent in the rich men like Seth Samsunderji. His character reminds us of Shakespeare's Shylock and Marlowe's Barabas. The portrait of the village constable Hoosiar Singh signifies the high-handedness of the British Raj.

The novel also depicts the Seth's four-fold activities: the money Seth, the Seth of politics, the official Seth and the Seth of religion. Bhattacharya also satirises the pseudo politicians wearing Gandhi caps. There is also depiction of the agitation and demonstration of the village women against the Seth for reduction in the price of cloth. There is also reference to the dishonest election methods conducted by the village Seth. The novel also reveals the Seth's craving for more and more money also. It depicts the villagers' belief in the horoscopes and astrological calculations. There is also reference to the Indians' belief in the existence of ghosts and devil. The novelist also satirises the extravagance of the villagers during marriage and other ceremonial functions. The novel also reveals Indian's belief in acquiring miraculous and magical powers by penance on the snowpeaks of the Himalayas and Kailash through the life and adventures of the minstrel.

The novel also refers to the advancement of science by mentioning penicillin and other inventions. There is also reference to the adoration of the Indians for a milched cow through the portrayal of the last phase of the cow Soondri. Another remarkable aspect is the prevalence of ceiling on all holdings including land. One mythological reference is the mentioning of *Parijat*, the tree in paradise blossoming flowers of gold.

The fifth novel *Shadow from Ladakh* depicts Indian life of the sixties. The Chinese invasion of India is the starting point for the conflict between the two communities, Gandhigram led by Satyajit Sen and Steeltown led by American trained Bhashkar Roy. But in the long run the novelist brings a resolution of the conflict in Sumita's marriage with Bhashkar. The novel shows the value and power of winning the hearts of opponents by the

Gandhian non-violent agitations and demonstrations. Besides, the novel reveals the modern necessity of steel as the only solace against the external aggression.

The novel reflects the new urges, the new spirit of India in the midst of struggles and crisis through the victory of Satyajit in his hunger strike against the government. Moreover, it depicts the bright aspect of the humanity of the Chinese children. The novel depicts the novelist's satire on the female elite for their spite and jealousy through the characters of Jhanak and Number Two. Jhanak is a girl who wants to live a full life of woman by not surrendering to any asceticism and austerity. Again, Number Two is a woman who is very jealous, self-conscious and self-centred.

The novel presents the image of sincerity, honesty, integrity and consciousness of national interest in the character of Bhashkar. There is also reference to women's participation in national problems as seen in Sumita's participation in the Peace Mission to Peking. The novel portrays Gandhigram as a microcosm of India. Everything happening there is happening everywhere in the country. National affairs are portrayed to be dominating the scene of action throughout the novel. The benevolence and kindness which are inherent qualities of the Indian race are shown through Bhashkar's loving treatment of the five little Chinese girls. There are also references to the novelist's adoration and appreciation of the Gandhian spiritualism and social ethics.

The latest and sixth novel *A Dream in Hawaii* depicts Indian life, social practices and their reactions and impacts on the American social life of the present-day. The novel depicts Indian faith in spiritualism and action free from desires for its fruit. Moreover, extrasensory perception is shown to be at the core of India's strength. Doing one's allotted work by leaving all its fruit to God, is vividly pictured in the novel. The novel has reference to the magnetic spiritual influence of four great Indian personalities—Gautama Buddha, Swami Vivekananda, Gurudev

Tagore and Mahatma Gandhi. Vivekananda's Vedantic concept of mind and his interest in contemporary man are also neatly referred to here. Through his personality is reflected the accepted norm of the discovery of Indian gurus first in the West.

Bhattacharya reveals the Indians' callous attitude towards Gandhi who is much respected and worshipped as a living presence in foreign countries. Besides, he emphasises upon the two forces of the gospel of Hare Krishna Movement and the concept of Transcendental Meditation both originated in India and swayed the lives of the Americans. Men and women are shown to live under the same roof in strict celibacy. Although they can marry, a woman in marriage is pledged to renounce sex when she begets two children or has passed her thirtieth year.

There is also a reference to Kamasutra, the ancient classic of India. The Americans consider it to be the best gospel for them. Again, the novel depicts Indian astrology which is exchanged for American technology. The existence of a religious *ashram* (temple) with a guru doing his *Sadhana* (meditation) in it is vividly shown. Many people are shown coming there to learn Yogic Disciplines in their quest for the ultimate Reality. There are also references to the popularity of Indian occult lore and rustic exorcism.

BHABANI BHATTACHARYA'S POPULARITY AT HOME AND ABROAD

Bhabani Bhattacharya is a gifted writer. With a brilliant academic career he has earned popularity not only in India but also abroad. Receiving B.A. (Hons.) degree from Patna University he went to London University from where he took the Ph.D. degree in Historical Research. Since he had a strong desire to have a glimpse of the universal poet Tagore he visited Santiniketan at the age of nineteen and met him there. Subsequently he won a prize in a literary competition held to select Tagore's poems for an anthology—'Chyanika.' From then onwards Bhabani became a close disciple of Tagore. During his student career in London he translated a good number of

Tagore's stories and sketches. At last he became the chief translator and the editor of the Tagore Centenary commemoration volume—"Towards the Universal Man."

Bhabani held many respectable positions in various fields. At one time he worked as Press Attache to the Indian Embassy in Washington, D.C. Besides, he worked as the Assistant Editor of the "Illustrated Weekly of India" during 1950-52. He occupied the secretaryship for the Tagore Commemorative Society, New Delhi in 1959-60. Next he ascended to the higher position of consultant in the Ministry of Education, New Delhi, in 1961-67. He was awarded the nation's prestigious—Sahitya Akademi Award in 1967 for his novel *Shadow from Ladakh.* Next year he was granted Ford Foundation fellowship to write the prestigious book "Gandhi the writer...." Next he became a member of the Sahitya Akademi Advisory Board.

Bhabani Bhattacharya's popularity abroad is not less than that he acquired in India. He travelled extensively. In 1951 he joined the team of the first Indian Cultural delegation of writers and scientists led by Dr. Baliga and visited Soviet Union as a member of the team. Next he attended (as a participant) the International Conference of Writers at Stockholm. Again, in 1959 he participated as a delegate in the Harvard International Seminar held at Cambridge, Massa-Chussets. Next year he attended a similar seminar at Tokyo, Japan. Next he lectured as a government guest in New Zealand and Australia in 1962. He gave lectures also in West Germany in 1963. During the "Festivals of Arts," Australia's biggest cultural festival, he attended a Writers' Conference at Adelaide. Later he was awarded prestigious awards by four universities of Australia and honoured him as one of the best Asian writers.

During 1969-70 he occupied the seat of Senior Specialist in the East-West Centre, Honolulu and since 1970 he has been a visiting professor in the University of Hawaii, Honolulu. In September, 1973 he joined the University of Washington, Seattle, as Walker-Ames-Professor, Mrs. Dorothy Shimer of the

Department of English, University of Hawaii wrote a book on Bhattacharya for Twayne Publishers of New York; which had been included in the famous world Authors Series. This is a great pride for Bhattacharya and a remarkable instance for his popularity throughout the world.

Moreover, his books have been translated into twenty-six languages of the world, sixteen of which are European. His wide range of experience in and around the world and his close association with men, manners and their personalities with which he grasps the innate significance of humanity, find their expressions in all his works. with all these qualities he is an outstanding Indo-Anglian novelist who has earned world-wide distinction and popularity.

REFERENCES

1. K.R. Chandrasekharan, *Bhabani Bhattacharya* (New Delhi: Arnold-Heinemann, 1974), 152.
2. R.K. Srivastava, *Bhattacharya's Prose Style*, quoted in "Perspectives on Bhabani Bhattacharya" (Ghaziabad: Vimal Prakashan, 1982), 113.
3. Meenakshi Mukherjee, *The Twice Born Fiction* (Delhi: Heinemann Educational Books, 1971), 181.
4. Chandrasekharan 150.
5. Srivastava 121.
6. Bhabani Bhattacharya, *Music for Mohini* (Delhi: Orient Paper backs, 1952), 37-38.
7. Bhabani Bhattacharya, *Shadow from Ladakh* (Delhi: Hind Pocket Books, 1966), 221.
8. Srivastava 124.
9. Srivastava 125.
10. V.K. Gokak, *The Concept of Indian Literature* (New Delhi: Munshiram Manoharlal, 1979), 112.
11. Gokak 112.
12. Samares C. Sanyal: *Indianness in Major Indo-Anglian Novels* (Bareilly: Prakash Book Depot, 1984), 258.
13. *World Literature Written in English*, Vol. 14, No. 2, Nov. 1975, 303-304 reproduced in S.C. Sanyal's *Indianness in Major Indo-Anglian Novel* (Bareilly: Prakash Book Depot., 1984), 265.

14. *Ibid.*, 266
15. Dr. R.K. Badal: *An Outline of Indo-Anglian Literature* (Bareilly: Prakash Book Depot., 1975), 53.
16. Bhabani Bhattacharya, *So Many Hungers*! (Bombay: Jaico, 1964), 172.
17. Bhabani Bhatacharya, *Music for Mohini* (Bombay: Jaico, 1964), 79.

7

CONCLUSION

The general survey of the Indo-Anglian fiction and the detailed analysis of the prominent political novels and the novel of Bhabani Bhattacharya, made in the foregoing chapters, have already shown the position and achievement of Bhabani Bhattacharya in the domain of Indian fiction. Strongly influenced by the Tagorean and the Gandhian ideals and inspired by the vision of a just social order, Bhattacharya wrote novels for social purpose and political value. Indeed, he portrayed full-blooded men and women, the peasant and the downtrodden as victims of social forces, but possessing the strength of re-making their motherland into a new India.

The study of the Indo-Anglian novels on varied themes,—social, political, nationalistic, diplomatic, cultural, etc.—of the periods before and after Independence has shown the significant place of Indian political novels and those of Bhabani Bhattacharya. The definitions, interpretations and analyses of "political novel" made by eminent scholars like Morris E. Speare, H.A.L. Fisher, Joseph L. Blotner, Irving Howe, etc. point to the concept of the term "political novel" as a novel expressing certain ideological preferences or describing existing political conditions. But according to Indian scholars: Mahadev L. Apte and Velcheru Narayan Rao, a "political novel" deals with a political ideology or has a political setting against which fictional characters are developed. The vast scope of political novel in Indian writing in English is seen through some of the important political novels thematically grouped as novels of: (l) armed rebellion, (2) Gandhian ideology, (3) partition riots and (4) post-Independence political issues. But the Indian content of these political novels has also created a context for the study of Bhattacharya's novels.

The critical analysis of the six novels of Bhattacharya has shown Bhattacharya's achievement. He has depicted contemporary social, political, economic and religious realities of India before and after her Independence. By delineating imaginative scenes as real and actual happenings, by using the themes of hunger and of political freedom, and by reflecting the rustic world he wrote *So Many Hungers!* Harmonisation of the contrastive aspects of human life in the Hindu society is the theme of *Music for Mohini. He who Rides a Tiger* records political, social, religious and economic aspects. But *A Goddess Named Gold* deals with the themes of freedom, hunger, synthesis and affirmation while *Shadow from Ladakh* is based on the theme of synthesis of Gandhism with Nehruism or Gandhian asceticism with Tagorean aestheticism. Clash of values of the East and the West, the relationship between art and religion and the synthesis of the old and the new are presented as the theme of *A Dream in Hawaii.*

Bhattacharya has propounded the theory of the social and moral function of art and has pleaded for reality and truth in literature. According to him, a novelist should not have a pre-conceived plot but should use contemporary events and social realities as subjects for writing novels. So the Bengal Famine of 1943 and the Quit India Movement of 1942 inspired him to write *So Many Hungers*! and *He who Rides a Tiger.* The synthesis of the old and the new values in Indian life urged him to write *Music for Mohini. A Goddess Named Gold* is concerned with the meaning of freedom while *Shadow from Ladakh* concerns with the Indo-China border conflict of 1962. He has explored an affirmative vision in all his novels. Denouncing asceticism and self-abnegation, he has pleaded for a full and joyous life in his *Music for Mohini, Shadow from Ladakh* and *A Dream in Hawaii.*

Bhattacharya is an innovator and a free user of the English language for artistic purpose. He has used an Indianised style, *i.e.*, literal translation and onomatopoeic words, to reflect Indian way of life and outlook and to convey Indian sensibility and culture. To use assertive sentence as interrogative sentence by adding a note of interrogation, to add the suffix *ful* to nouns, to use Hindi words and repetitive words or phrases, to drop 'to be' verb, and to use irony, humour, natural dialogue, metaphors, fragmentary sentences, etc. form the core of his artistic and mature linguistic style.

We have seen Bhattacharya's authentic tone and Indian-ness through the common theme, traditional technique and typical Indian language of his novels. A gifted writer with a brilliant academic career and a holder of many respectable positions in various fields in India and abroad, he earned an international popularity.

In conclusion, it can be unhesitatingly stated that because of his significant contributions in theme, form and style, Bhabani Bhattacharya is one of the most outstanding Indo-Anglian novelists.

Bibliography

[A] A CHRONOLOGICAL LIST OF INDIAN POLITICAL NOVELS IN ENGLISH

K.C. Dutta, *A Journal of Fortyeight Hours of the Year 1945*. Calcutta: n.p., 1835.

S.C. Dutt, *Republic of Orissa: Annals from the pages of the Twentieth Century*. Calcutta: n.p., 1845.

——, *The Young Zamindar*. London: n.p., 1883.

S.K. Ghosh, *The Prince of Destiny; the New Krishna*. London: Rebman, 1909.

S.M. Mitra, *Hindupore*. London: Luzac, 1909.

R.N. Tagore, *The Home and the World* (Eng. tr.). Madras: MacMillan & Co., 1919.

——, *Gora* (Eng. tr.). Calcutta: MacMillan & Co., 1923.

Dhan Gopal Mukerjee, *My Brother's Face*. London: Thornton Butterworth, 1926.

K.S. Venkataramani, *Murugan, The Tiller*. London: Simpkin, Marshall, Hamilton and Kent, 1927.

A. Subramanyam, *Indira Devi*. n.p. 1930.

K.S. Venkataramani, *Kandan, The Patriot*. Madras: Svetraya Ashrama, 1932.

H. Das Frieda, *Into The Sun*. n.p., 1933.

M.R. Anand, *Untouchable*. London: Lawrence and Wishart, 1933.

——, *Coolie*. London: Hutchinson's International Authors.

K.S. Nagarajan, *Athawar House*. Madras: Higginbotham's, 1937.

Raja Rao, *Kanthapura*. London: George Allen & Unwin Ltd., 1938.

Ahmad Ali, *Twilight in Delhi*. Bombay: n.p., 1940.

M.R. Anand, *The Sword and the Sickle*. Bombay: Kutub Publishers, 1942.

K.A. Abbas, *Tomorrow is Ours*. Delhi: n.p. , 1943.

D.F. Karaka, *We Never Die*. London: Thacker and Co., 1944.

C.N. Zutsi, *Motherland: An Expository Novel of Modern India*, n.p., 1944.

K.A. Abbas, *Defeat for Death*. n.p., 1944.

Aamir Ali, *Conflict*. Bombay: National Information and Publications, 1947.

Bhabani Bhattacharya, *So Many Hungers!* Bombay: Hind Kitab, 1947.

N.S. Phadke, *Leaves in the August Wind*. n.p., 1947.

R.N. Tagore, *Four Chapters* (Eng. tr.). Calcutta: Vishvabharati, 1950.

Venu Chitale, *In Transit*. Bombay: Hind Kitab, 1950.

Zeenut Futehally, *Zohra*. Bombay: Hind Kitab, 1951.

Attia Hossain, *Sunlight on a Broken Column*. London: Chatto & Windus, 1951.

M.R. Anand, *Private Life of an Indian Prince*. London: Hutchinson's International Authors, 1953.

K.A. Abbas, *Inquilab*. Bombay: Jaico Publications, 1955.

Lambert Mascarenhas, *Sorrowing Lies My Land*. n.p., 1955.

R.K. Narayan, *Waiting for the Mahatma*. East Lansing: Michigan State University Press, 1955.

N.S. Phadke, *The Whirlwind*. n.p., 1956.

Arthur Lall, *The House at Adampur*. Bombay: Pearl Publications, 1956.

Khushwant Singh, *Train to Pakistan*. London: Chatto & Windus, 1956.

Kamala Markandaya, *Some Inner Fury*. London: Putnam & Company, 1957.

Nayantara Sahgal, *A Time to be Happy*. Bombay: Jaico Publications, 1958.

Khuswant Singh, *I Shall Not Hear the Nightingale*. London: John Calder, 1959.

B. Rajan, *The Dark Dancer*. London: Heinemann, 1959.

Manohar Malgonkar, *Distant Drum*. Bombay: Asia Publishing House, 1960.

S. Menon Marath, *Wound of Spring*. London: Denis Dobson, 1960.

K. Nagarajan, *Chronicles of Kedaram*. Bombay: Asia Publishing House, 1961.

Manohar Malgonkar, *Combat of Shadows*. London: Hamish Hamilton, 1962.

Mulk Raj Anand, *Death of a Hero*. Bombay: Kutub Popular, 1963.

Manohar Malgonkar, *The Princes*. London: Hamish Hamilton, 1963.

——, *A Bend in the Ganges*. London: Hamish Hamilton, 1964.

Nayantara Sahgal, *This Time of Morning*. London: Victor Gollanez, 1965.

Bhabani Bhattacharya, *Shadow from Ladakh*. London: W.H. Allun, 1966.

R.K. Narayan, *Vendor of Sweets*. Mysore: Indian Thought Publication, 1967.

Nayantara Sahgal, *Storm in Chandigarh*. Delhi: Hind Pocket Books, 1969.

——, *The Day in Shadow*. Delhi: Vikas Publications, 1971.

Raj Gill, *The Rape*. Delhi: Orient Paperback, 1974.

Chaman Nahal, *Azadi*. Delhi: Orient Paperback, 1975.

Nayantara Sahgal, *A Situation in New Delhi*. Delhi: Orient-Paperback, 1977.

Chaman Nahal, *The Crown and the Loincloth*. New Delhi: Vikas Publishing House, 1981.

Salman Rushdie, *Midnight's Children*. London: Picador, Pan Books, 1981.

[B] CRITICAL STUDIES ON POLITICAL NOVELS (INDO-ANGLIAN)

Apte, Mahdev L., "The Political Novel in Marathi" in *Politics and the Novel in India*, ed. Jogendra K. Malik. New Delhi: Orient Longman, 1978.

Blotner, Joseph L., *The Political Novel.* New York: Doubleday, 1955.

Coppola, Carlo, "Politics and the Novel in India: Perspective," in *Politics and the Novel in India.* Ed. Jogendra K. Malik. New Delhi: Orient Longman, 1978.

Fisher, H.A.L., "The Political Novel" Quoted by Gordon Milne, *The American Political Novel.* Norman: University of Oklahoma Press, 1966.

Irving Howe, *Politics and the Novel.* New York: Horizon Press, 1957.

Naik, M.K., *Dimensions of Indian English Literature.* New Delhi: Sterling Publishers Pvt. Ltd., 1984.

Rama Jha, *Gandhian Thought and Indo-Anglian Novelist.* Delhi: Chanakya Publications, 1983.

Speare, Morris E., *The Political Novel: Its Development in England and America.* New York: Oxford University Press, 1924.

Velcheru Narayan Rao: "The Political Novel in Telegu," in *Politics and the Novel in India,* ed. Jogendra K. Malik. New Delhi: Orient Longman, 1978.

[C] NOVELS OF BHABANI BHATTACHARYA

A Dream in Hawaii. Delhi: Macmillan India Ltd., 1978.

A Goddess Named Gold. New York: Crown Publishers, 1960.

He Who Rides a Tiger. Delhi: Hind Pocket Books, 1955.

Music for Mohini. Delhi: Orient Paperbacks, 1952.

Shadow from Ladakh. Delhi: Hind Pocket Books, 1966.

So Many Hungers! Bombay: Hind Kitab, 1947.

(D) OTHER WRITINGS OF BHABANI BHATTACHARYA

"Baseless Prejudice Against Indians Writing English" in *The Statesman*. New Delhi: August 1968.

"Bridge Between the Peoples," in *India and South East Asia: Proceedings of a Seminar*. New Delhi: Indian Council for Cultural Relations, 1966, 99-101.

"City of Cities Now Called, Callous" in *India: A Survey Compiled from the Times*. London: Times Publishing Co., 1962.

Contemporary Indian Short Stories, Series II (edited). New Delhi: Sahitya Akademi, 1967.

"Europe-Behind the Veil." series of articles in *The Hindu*. Madras: 1930.

Gandhi the Writer: The Image As It Grew. New Delhi: National Book Trust, 1969.

Golden Boat, The. Bombay: Jaico Publishing House, 1955.

"Hawkers in an Indian Noon" in *Asia Magazine*. New York: 1935.

"Hollow Arbiters of the, Writer's Destiny" in *The Statesman*. New Delhi: May, 1968.

"How I Wrote *So Many Hungers!*" in *Letteraturnaya Gazetta*. Moscow: 1951.

"In London Today" in *The Hindu*. Madras: 1930.

Indian Cavalcade, Bombay: Nalanda Publications, 1948.

"Indo-Anglian" in *The Novel in Modern India*. Bombay: P.E.N. India Centre, 1964, 41-48.

"Lifelong Dynamism" in *Hemisphere*. Sydney, 1961.

"Literature and Social Reality" in *The Aryan Path*. Bombay: 1939.

"Nature of Wisdom" in *Abbottempo*. North Chicago: Abbot Universal Ltd., 1970.

"People of the Village Change Their Theme, The" in *The Times*. London: Jan. 23, 1961.

Socio-Political Currents in Bengal: A 19th Century Perspective. New Delhi: Vikas Publishing House, 1980.

Some Memorable Yesterdays. Patna: Pustak Bhandar, 1941.

"Tagore as a Novelist" in *Rabindranath Tagor 1861—1961: A Centenary Volume*. New Delhi: Sahitya Akademi, 1961, 96-101.

"This Week in History" in *The Hindu*. Madras, 1935.

Towards Universal Man. Bombay: Asia Publishing House, 1961.

[E] CRITICAL STUDIES ON BHABANI BHATTACHARYA AND INDO-ANGLIAN FICTION

Anand, M.R., *The King Emperor' s English*. Bombay: n.d.

——, *The Big Heart*. London: Hutchinson's International Authors, 1945.

Asnani, Shyam M., *Critical Response to Indian English Fiction*. Delhi: Mittal Publications, 1985.

Atma Ram, *Essays on Indian English Literature*. Aurangabad: Parimal Prakashan, 1984.

Badal, R.K., *Indo-Anglian Literature: An Outline*. Bareilly: Prakash Book Depot., 1975.

Balarama Gupta, G.S., *Mulk Raj Anand: A Study of His Fiction in Humanist Perspective*. Bareilly: Prakash Book Depot, 1974.

Bhattacharya, P.C., *Indo-Anglian Literature and the Works of Raja Rao*. Delhi: Atma Ram and Sons, 1983.

Bhupal Singh, *Brief Survey of Anglo-Indian Fiction*. London: Oxford University Press, 1934.

Chandrasekharan,K.R., *Bhabani Bhattacharya*. New Delhi: Arnold-Heinemann, 1974.

David Mc Cutchion, *Indian Writing in English*. Calcutta: Writers Workshop, 1963.

Derret, M.E., *The Modern Indian Novel in English: A Comparative Approach*. Brussels: L' Institute de Sociologie University Libre de Bruxelles, 1966.

Dorothy Blair Shimer, *Bhabani Bhattacharya*. New York: Twayne Publishers, 1975.

Dorothy Spencer, M., *Indian Fiction in English*. Philadelphia: University of Pennsylvania Press, 1960.

Gokak, V.K., *English in India: Its Present and Future*. Bombay: Asia Publishing House, 1964.

——, *Modern Indian Languages*. New Delhi: Publication Division, Ministry of Information and Broadcasting, 1957.

——, *The Concept of Indian Literature*. New Delhi: Munshiram Manoharla1, 1979.

Goyal, B.S., *Culture and Commitment: Aspects of Indian Literature in English*. Meerut: Shalabh Book House, 1984.

Harrex, S.C., *The Fire and the Offering*, Vol. I. Calcutta: Writers Workshop, 1977.

Hari Mohan Prasad, *Response: Recent Revelations of Indian Fiction in English*. Bareilly: Prakash Book Depot, 1983.

Harish Raizada, *The Lotus and the Rose: Indian Fiction in English*. Aligarh, Muslim University, 1978.

Iqbal Bakhtiyar (ed.), *The Novel in Modern India*. Bombay: P.E.N. Centre, 1964.

Iyengar, K.R.S., *Indian Writing in English*. New Delhi: Sterling Publishers, 3rd edition, 1983.

——, *Contemporary Indian Literature, A Symposium*. Delhi: Sahitya Akademi, 1981.

Joshi, K.N. and Syamala Rao, B., *Studies in Indo-Anglian Literature*. Bareilly: Prakash Book Depot, 1979-80.

Krishna Kripalani, *Modern Indian Literature*. Bombay: Nirmal Sadananda, 1963.

Krishna Rao, A.V., *The Indo-Anglian Novel and the Changing Tradition*. Mysore: Rao and Raghavan, 1972.

Meena Shirwadkar, *The Image of Woman in the Indo-Anglian Novel*. Delhi: Sterling Publishers, 1979.

Mehta, P.P., *Indo-Anglian Fiction: An Assessment*. Bareilly: Prakash Book Depot, 1979.

Melwani Murli Das, *Themes in Indo-Anqlian Literature*. Bareilly: Prakash Book Depot, 1977.

Mukherjee, Meenakshi, *The Twice-Born Fiction*. New Delhi: Arnold-Heinemann, 1971.

Naik, M.K., *A History of Indian English Literature*. New Delhi: Sahitya Akademi, 1982.

Naik, Amur & Desai (Ed.), *Critical Essays on Indian Writing in English*. Dharwar: Karnatak University, 1968.

Narasimhaiah, C.D. (Ed.), *Fiction and the Reading Public in India*. Mysore: Mysore University, 1969.

——, *The Swan and the Eagle*. Simla: Indian Institute of Advanced Studies, 1969.

Paul Verghese, C., *Problems of Indian Creative Writers in English*. Bombay: Somaiya Publications, 1971.

Radhakrishnan, N., *Indo-Anglian Fiction: Major Trends and Themes*. Madras: Emerald Publishers, 1984.

Raja Rao, *Preface to Cat and Shakespeare*. Delhi: Hind Pocket Books, Pvt. Ltd., 1971.

Sarma, G.P., *Nationalism in Indo-Anglian Fiction*; New Delhi: Sterling Publishers, Pvt. Ltd., 1978.

Santha Krishnaswamy, *The Woman in Indian Fiction in English*. New Delhi: Ashish Publishing House, 1984.

Samares C. Sanyal, *Indianness in Major Indo-Anglian Novel*. Bareilly: Prakash Book Depot, 1984.

Sharma, K.K., *Bhabani Bhattacharya: His Vision and Themes*. Delhi: Abhinav Publications, 1979.

Srivastava, R.K., *Perspectives on Bhabani Bhattacharya*. Ghaziabad: Vimal Prakashan, 1982.

Stephen Ignatius Hemenway, *The Novel in India, Vol. 2. The Indo-Anglian Novel*. Calcutta: Writers Workshop, 1975.

Syamala Rao, B., *Bhabani Bhattacharya and His Works*. Bareilly: Student Store, n.d.

Williams, H.M., *Indo-Anglian Literature* (l800-1970): *A Survey*. Delhi: Orient Longman Ltd., 1976.

[F] ARTICLES ON BHABANI BHATTACHARYA

Bhabani Bhattacharya: "Literature and Social Reality: *The Aryan Path*," xxvi, No. 9, Sept. 1955, 392-95.

Cromwell Crawford: "Bhabani Bhattacharya: A Meditating Man," in *Perspectives on Bhabani Bhattacharya,* ed. R.K. Srivastava. Ghaziabad: Vimal Prakashan, 1982, 7-19.

Dhawan, R.K., "Bhattacharya's Narrative Technique," in *Perspectives on Bhabani Bhattacharya.* ed. R.K. Srivastava. Ghaziabad: Vimal Prakashan, 1982, 185-99.

Elena Kalinnikova, "The Problems of Bhabani Bhattacharya's Novels," in *Perspectives on Bhabani Bhattacharya,* ed. R.K. Srivastava. Ghaziabad: Vimal Prakashan, 1982, 101-10.

Harcharn Boparai, "The Achievement of Bhabani Bhattacharya," in *Perspectives on Bhabani Bhattacharya.* ed. R.K. Srivastava. Ghaziabad: Vimal Prakashan, 1982, 200-16.

Harish Raizada, "Fiction as Allegory: Novels of Bhabani Bhattacharya," in *Perspectives on Bhabani Bhattacharya,* ed. R.K. Srivastava. Ghaziabad: Vimal Prakashan, 1982, 83-100.

JIWE, Vol. 3 No. 2, July, 1975. Ed. Balarama Gupta, G.S. Krishna Rao, A.V., "He Who Rides a Tiger," in *Perspectives on Bhabani Bhattacharya,* ed. R.K. Srivastava. Ghaziabad: Vimal Prakashan, 1982, 141-48.

Smt. Lila Ray, "Bhabani Bhattacharya: A Profile," in *Indian Literature,* Vol. xi, No. 2, April-July, 1968, 73-76.

Marlene Fisher, "The Women in Bhattacharya's Novels," in *Perspectives on Bhabani Bhattacharya,* ed. R.K. Srivastava. Ghaziabad: Vimal Prakashan, 1982, 66-81.

Narasingh Srivastava, "Symbol and Allegory in A Goddess Named Gold," in *Perspectives on Bhabani Bhattacharya,* ed. R.K. Srivastava. Ghaziabad: Vimal Prakashan, 1982, 149-65.

Paul Verghese C., "Raja Rao, Mulk Raj Anand, Narayan and Others," in *Indian Writing Today,* Vol. 7, No. 3, Jan-Mar. 1969, 31-38.

——, "The Problems of Indian Novelist in English," in *The Banasthali Patrika,* No. 12, Jan. 1969, ed. Rameswar Gupta.

Prema Nandakumar, "The Achievement of the Indo-Anglian Novelist," *The Literary Criterion*, Vol. VI, No. 1, Winter, 1 961.

Ramakrishna, D., "Academics and Yogis: Reflections on the Recent Indo-English Fiction," *JIWE*, Vol. 7, No. 2, July, 1979, 19-25.

Sarma, P.P., "Bhabani Bhattacharya: Artist/Propagandist," in *Perspectives on Bhabani Bhattacharya*, ed. R.K. Srivastava. Ghaziabad: Vimal Prakashan, 1982, 41-51.

Srivastava, R.K., "Bhattacharya's Prose Style," in *Perspectives on Bhabani Bhattacharya*, ed. R.K. Srivastava. Ghaziabad: Vimal Prakashan, 1982, 111-125.

Sudhakar Joshi, "An Evening With Bhabani," *The Sunday Standard*, 27 April, 1969.

World Literatures Written in English, Vol. 14, No. 2, Nov. 1975.

The Western Humanities Review, Vol. 15, No. 4, Autumn, 1961.

Index